THE REAL READ

Slightly Foxed

'the cat who was cleopatra'

NO.72 WINTER 2021

Editors: Gail Pirkis & Hazel Wood
Editorial & submissions: Anna Kirk
Marketing & publicity: Steph Allen, Jennie Harrison Bunning & Hattie Summers
Subscriptions, orders & bookshops: Jess Dalby & Iona Glen

Cover illustration: Neil Gower, *Hunter's Moon*

Neil Gower is an internationally acclaimed graphic artist, best known for his book jackets (Bill Bryson, William Golding) and literary cartography (Kazuo Ishiguro, Jilly Cooper, Simon Armitage). As befits an artist, he was born into black and now inhabits white: respectively the coal of the 1960s Rhondda Valley and the chalk trails of the South Downs. He lives in Lewes and – when global events permit – Kreuzberg, Berlin. Marking a shift from distilling the words of others into paint, his first collection of poetry, *Meet Me in Palermo*, was published in September by the Frogmore Press. For more of his work and to contact him see his website (www.neilgower.com) or follow him on Instagram (@neiljgower).

Design by Octavius Murray
Layout by Andrew Evans
Colophon and tailpiece by David Eccles

© The contributors 2021

Published by Slightly Foxed Limited
53 Hoxton Square
London N1 6PB

tel 020 7033 0258
email office@foxedquarterly.com
www.foxedquarterly.com

Slightly Foxed is published quarterly in early March, June, September and December

Annual subscription rates (4 issues)
UK and Ireland £48; Overseas £56

Single copies of this issue can be bought for £12.50 (UK) or £14.50 (Overseas)

All back issues in printed form are also available

ISBN 978-1-910898-52-9
ISSN 1742-5794

Printed and bound by Smith Settle, Yeadon, West Yorkshire

Contents

Contents

John Watson

The Slightly Foxed Podcast

A new episode of our podcast is available on the 15th of every month. To listen, visit www.foxedquarterly.com/pod or search for Slightly Foxed on Audioboom, Apple Podcasts or your podcast app.

Subscriber Benefits

Slightly Foxed can obtain any books reviewed in this issue, whether new or second-hand. To enquire about a book, to access the digital edition of *Slightly Foxed* or to view a list of membership benefits, visit www.foxedquarterly.com/members or contact the office: 020 7033 0258/office@foxedquarterly.com.

From the Editors

Wednesday 29 September was a red-letter day for us – the first time for eighteen months that we'd got together under one roof to record the *Slightly Foxed* podcast. Since the first lockdown in March 2020 we'd been sitting at home each month at our separate desks waiting – usually a touch nervously in our case as we're neither of us entirely confident when it comes to anything technical – to see if we'd made the connection with Philippa our presenter in Cambridge and Lynne our producer in Cheshire.

Thanks to them, the podcasts have usually gone without a hitch, but it was so cheering to be together again in Hoxton Square and to meet our guests in person, on this occasion to talk about the graphic novel with the wonderful Posy Simmonds and the writer Paul Gravett. It's well worth a listen if you haven't already heard it. Altogether we felt distinctly festive, and now we're looking forward – with fingers crossed – to a much more relaxed and sociable Christmas.

There could hardly be a more fitting book for the season than our latest Slightly Foxed Edition, *The Wine Lover's Daughter* by Anne Fadiman, whose earlier book, *Ex Libris*, we praised in the opening piece in our very first issue eighteen years ago. As Adam Sisman says (see p.14), the title is something of a misnomer: *The Wine Loving Father* would be more apt for this affectionate but clear-eyed memoir in which the American writer remembers her convivial and amusing father, a complicated self-made Jew from Brooklyn with a passion for wine who, though moving in the best literary circles and heaped with honours by the end of his life, never felt he was quite good enough. It's not just a book for wine buffs either, but one that breathes the atmosphere of a more spacious era in American literary life.

From father and daughter to father and son. Between the spring of 1945 and the autumn of 1947 the artist Charles Phillipson wrote a series of 150 illustrated letters to his young son Michael, who had just started school. These delightful, quirky letters, designed to whet Michael's appetite for reading, were done when Charles had already been diagnosed with multiple sclerosis, but they are full of the lightness and humour he still found in everyday situations, and full of encouragement for Michael's own efforts. Preserved by his wife after his death in 1974 these *Letters to Michael*, which we published in November, give a most touching picture of the relationship between a father and his young son.

And finally, for those many of you who have loved the Adrian Bell trilogy describing his life between the wars on a Suffolk farm, a reminder of another, recently published, treat. From 1950 to 1980 Bell wrote a popular column for his local paper, the *Eastern Daily Press*, 1,600 atmospheric little essays which vividly catch the fleeting moments that made up his life in the rural Suffolk he loved and knew so well. Surprisingly, very few have since been reprinted, but now they can be enjoyed again in *A Countryman's Winter Notebook*, a seasonal selection by Richard Hawking, with an introduction by Bell's son Martin and charming illustrations by Beth Knight. We hope it will be the first of these little seasonal selections.

We hope too above all, dear readers, that your Christmas season will be a peaceful and happy one. We send you our very best wishes and thanks, as ever, for your exceptional loyalty which has kept us afloat in these difficult times.

GAIL PIRKIS & HAZEL WOOD

the cat who was cleopatra

WILLIAM PALMER

In the 1920s, some of the more daring modernist poets further liberated their already metre-free verse by abandoning capital letters and conventional punctuation. One unfortunate poet had little choice. His diminutive size and the configuration of his limbs determined the way in which he was forced to write. Here he is, working at night on a typewriter in a deserted newspaper office:

> He would climb painfully upon the framework of the machine and cast himself with all his force upon a key, head downwards, and his weight and the impact of the blow were just sufficient to operate the machine, one slow letter after another. He could not work the capital letters and he had a great deal of difficulty in operating the mechanism that shifts the paper so that a fresh line may be started . . . After about an hour of this frightfully difficult literary labor he fell to the floor exhausted.

The piece of paper left in the machine is examined. It reads:

> expression is the need of my soul
> i was once a vers libre bard
> but i died and my soul went into the body of a
>   cockroach
> it has given me a new outlook upon life

Don Marquis's *archy and mehitabel* (1927) is out of print but there is an excellent compendium of it and the other Archy books (*archys life of mehitabel*, 1933; and *archy does his part*, 1935) available from Everyman: *The Best of Archy and Mehitabel* (2011) · Hb · 224pp · £9.99 · ISBN 9781841597911.

This is how Don Marquis introduces his creation Archy – or 'archy' as the typing cockroach is forced to describe himself. Most cockroaches are tough little creatures, but Archy soon reveals himself as sensitive, rather anxious and bullied by another ex-poet, now reincarnated as a rat, who is jealous of Archy's work and 'after he has read it he sneers/ and then he eats it'.

But Archy has seen that the man who uses the typewriter during the day is interested in what is left in his machine overnight and is encouraged by this new audience: 'i will write you a series of poems showing how things look'. These are the comic poems that make up *archy and mehitabel*, first published in 1927, and largely concerning Archy's friendship with a female cat, the magnificent if rather battered and gamey Mehitabel. He discusses reincarnation with her:

talking it over in a
friendly way who were you
mehitabel i asked her i was
cleopatra once she said well i said i
suppose you lived in a palace you bet
she said

Mehitabel's most common expressions for dealing with life's vicissitudes are a dismissive 'wot the hell archy wot the hell' and the defiant 'toujour gai archy toujour gai' whenever one of her romances falls to pieces. She has an extensive past in affairs of the heart, which stretches back through many transmigrations from one existence to another. But when Archie asks her about Mark Antony and Caesar, she doesn't recognize their names; after all, as she says, she has met 'so many prominent gentlemen i/ won't lie to you or stall i/ do get my dates mixed up sometimes'.

There's more of the Bronx about Mehitabel than there is of Ancient Egypt, and her adventures form the funniest and most enduring of Archy's poems. True, Mehitabel does treat her chronicler a little roughly sometimes, once coming close, in an abstracted moment, to eating him. But then, it's a dangerous world they inhabit, based on a whole hierarchy of predators – in one of Archy's modernized Aesop fables, 'the robin and the worm', there is a protest against fate as the worm is eaten by the robin. While being digested

> he exclaimed
> i am losing my personal
> identity as a worm
> > my individuality
> > is melting away from me
> > odds craw i am becoming
> > part and parcel of
> > this bloody robin

The robin, sated with the worm, sings a sweet song, and fails to notice Mehitabel sneaking up behind him:

> she pounced just as he
> had extended his larynx
> in a melodious burst of
> thanksgiving and
> > he went the way of all
> > flesh fish and good red herring

Mehitabel, in a way probably near the truth of how cats actually think, philosophically considers the fate of the worm and the robin:

> they breakfast in heaven
> all s well with the world
> how true that is
> > and even yet his song
> > echoes in the haunted
> > woodland of my midriff

The seven pages of 'the worm and the robin' never flag in their intense dark comedy, pointing out that the higher a creature is in the food chain, the more complicated its adaptation of moral sense to its own survival. That morally complicated creature, the human being, makes only rare appearances. The most sophisticated of the animals are probably the lovers of Mehitabel. She is forever being picked up by some 'slick looking tom' who lives with his rich owners in a fine house and promises love and access to the pantry and icebox. One night, Mehitabel is foully double-crossed:

> just as we had got
> the icebox door open and were
> about to sample the cream
> in comes his mistress
> why fluffy she says to this slicker
> the idea of you making
> friends with a horrid creature like that

And, of course, the tom pretends not to know his companion of the night. He turns and attacks her and, aided by the lady of the house and a cook with a broom, Mehitabel is rousted out of the door. The revenge she takes after lying for two days and nights in the shrubbery is savagely funny – full of elegantly blistering reproach as astonishingly bloody violence is inflicted on this particular 'social swell'.

Don Marquis was born in 1878 and died in 1937. Today he is only widely known for his books about Archy, Mehitabel and assorted other creatures. But he also wrote an enormous amount of daily and weekly journalism, novels, collections of short stories, Hollywood screenplays, serious and comic poetry, and a play, *The Old Soak* (Marquis was a heavy drinker), that ran for 325 performances on Broadway in the early 1920s. (Other plays, religious or historical, came to nothing.)

Like most wits Marquis was not a happy man and, like most voluminous writers, only a fraction of what he wrote is now read. Some critics have said that much of his work in other fields is unfairly neglected. Rather like Arthur Conan Doyle, who felt that Sherlock Holmes had overshadowed his historical novels, Marquis came to feel the same about Archy. Certainly, he believed that his prodigious output as a newspaper columnist had got in the way of a major serious novel he had worked on for years but never managed to complete. In 1928, at the age of 50, he wrote in a letter to a friend: 'I have never told anybody, how deep and abiding my professional disappointments are . . . Except in brief and fragmentary things I have never displayed the powers I have, or developed them.' Significantly, in the late 1920s a younger generation of novelists, including Fitzgerald and Hemingway, had already won fame for their work: Marquis must have felt that he had been left on the shelf, his only fame coming from a book of comic verse about a cockroach and a libidinous cat.

There were other, deeper causes of despair. Marquis had clawed his way out of youthful poverty and a series of menial jobs to become one of America's leading journalists, and a persistent fear of failure led him to take on too many commitments. His health was damaged by overwork and, perhaps, by his drinking. His personal life had the unremitting darkness of a Greek tragedy. In 1909, he married Reina Melcher. They had a son and daughter; the son died aged 5, and Reina died in 1923. Marquis remarried in 1926. The daughter of his first marriage died five years later, aged just 15. Marquis himself suffered a devastating stroke in 1936, and his second wife died that same year. Marquis followed her in 1937.

So perhaps we can forgive Marquis for the wry disdain with which his poet, Archy, treats the meaning of life:

> i once heard the survivors
> of a colony of ants
> that had been partially
> obliterated by a cow s foot
> seriously debating

the intention of the gods
towards their civilization

Such complacency is found elsewhere in Archy's animal world. In 'warty bliggens, the toad', Warty spends his days sitting under a toadstool that he believes was created solely for his comfort, to shelter him from sun and rain:

do not tell me
said warty bliggens
that there is not a purpose
in the universe
the thought is blasphemy . . .

to what act of yours
do you impute
this interest on the part
of the creator
of the universe
i asked him
why is it that you
are so greatly favored

ask rather
said warty bliggens
what the universe
has done to deserve me

Luckily for us, most of the characters Archy meets and immortalizes are full of energy and tell wonderful stories of their previous and present lives: spiders, flies, hornets, a parrot who knew Shakespeare in a past existence, even a tarantula who arrives by ship from South America in a bunch of bananas and proceeds to terrify the local community until dealt with by Freddy the Rat. Unfortunately, Freddy succumbs in their epic battle and is buried with full military honours in a nearly clean dustbin.

But the chief glory of the collection is the indestructible, endlessly promiscuous Mehitabel. The book ends with cockroach and cat enjoying a trip to London and Paris. As usual Mehitabel finds a soulmate and goes to live with him in (where else?) the catacombs of Paris: an 'outcast feline/ who calls himself/ francois villon', who regales Mehitabel with poetry of a thoroughly Villonesque nature (excellently rendered by Archy in most skilfully handled metre and rhyme).

Archy looks on with awe at the cat's latest romance. He himself, a warm-hearted, amiable creature, has only one real ambition, one shared by many others in life:

> say boss please lock the shift
> key tight some night
> i would like to tell the story of
> my life all in capital
> letters
>
> archy

WILLIAM PALMER's latest book, *In Love with Hell*, a study of alcohol in the lives and work of eleven writers, was published earlier this year. The illustrations in this article are by George Herriman.

CAPITALS AT LAST

A Vintage Life

ADAM SISMAN

Anne Fadiman's memoir of her father originated as one of several ideas for an article that she pitched to an editor at *Harper's* magazine. 'I think I could tell the story of my father's life and character through wine,' she proposed.

'The Oenophile's Daughter!' he exclaimed.

His suggested title was jettisoned when they discovered that hardly anyone else knew what 'oenophile' meant, or how to spell or pronounce it. And soon afterwards the editor parted ways with *Harper's*. But the idea took root; and Anne Fadiman realized that she wanted to write a book on the subject, not an article. In many ways her eventual title, *The Wine Lover's Daughter*, is a misnomer; *The Wine Loving Father* is a more obvious description – though of course, in telling us about her father, she also tells us about herself.

First published in 2017, her delightful book has not until now been available outside America. And it should be, because this is a minor classic. Though a distinctively American story, it is one which will resonate with fathers and daughters everywhere – which, come to think of it, includes most of us. A friend recommended the book to me; I confess that I had not heard of Anne Fadiman before, but now that I have been introduced to her writing, I shall certainly seek out more.

Clifton Fadiman took his first sip of wine, a white Graves, in 1927, in the Bon Marché department store in Paris. Then in his early twenties, he had travelled across the Atlantic in pursuit of his errant first wife, an expedition he would later recount to his family as a mock-heroic epic, 'The Retrieval of Polly'. The marriage did not last; but his new love, for wine, would be passionate and lifelong. He studied wine and bought the best vintages he could afford.

Fadiman never became a wine snob, in the sense of speaking or writing pretentiously about it. He loved wine for a number of reasons, some of which he enunciated in an essay published thirty years after that first sip, entitled 'A Brief History of a Love Affair': because drinking it was companionable, and because it provided sensory pleasure; because wine was complex, and because it was hierarchical, in the sense that some wines were 'first-rate' and some were not; because it was an intelligible field of study; and because it was not vulgar. And also (though he would never have admitted this) because it wasn't Jewish.

When Anne Fadiman wrote a piece for *Life* magazine to mark her father's eightieth birthday, he told her that he would prefer her not to mention the fact that he was a Jew. 'If I had no legs and you wrote a piece about me,' he said, 'I would prefer you write about me as a man.' For him, being Jewish was like having a handicap.

Worldly and amusing, and a gifted mimic, 'Kip' Fadiman was a successful author, critic, translator, columnist, publisher and broadcaster, valued both for his erudite charm and his good-natured wordplay ('between a wok and a hot plate'). Several of these jobs he held simultaneously; in fact he filled so many roles that he was once described as a 'celebrated multihyphenate'. With the air of having read everything ever written, he was a prime example of the witty and educated raconteurs and pundits chosen to host American radio and television shows in the mid-twentieth century.

His break in publishing had come when he secured an interview with Max Schuster, co-founder of the then new and dynamic publishing house Simon & Schuster. On being asked 'What makes you think you might be helpful to us?', Fadiman had presented Schuster with a folder containing a typed list of no fewer than *one hundred* ideas for books. He was made editor-in-chief, at the age of only 28. The next year he was appointed to run the book pages for *The New*

Clifton and Anne Fadiman, in her office at *Life*, 1984

Yorker. He became famous as host of the popular radio show *Information Please*, which at its wartime peak attracted 15 million listeners across America. For many years he was on the board of the Book-of-the-Month Club, and in old age received a National Book Award for his Distinguished Contribution to American Letters.

Yet despite all his accomplishments, Fadiman continued to see himself as an outsider. He contemplated writing an autobiographical book-length essay, addressed to his children, to be read after his death, called 'Outside, Looking In'. His children were aware of his sense of insecurity. 'We all knew he felt like a man who has been admitted by mistake to a gentlemen's club and, as soon as he is discovered, will be booted out the service entrance.' He joked about his humble beginnings – but beneath the self-deprecatory persona 'some ugly things were laid bare: anxiety, humiliation, shame'. Anne Fadiman depicts her father as one of a generation of self-alienated Jews: secular intellectuals whose denial of their Jewish identity was so absolute as to seem in retrospect almost farcical.

Fadiman was a self-invented man, whose talent and industriousness had enabled him to shake off his modest origins. The son of a nurse and a druggist, he had grown up in Brooklyn, 'a century before it became fashionable . . . crowded with immigrants and smelling of garbage and noisy with street fights'. In an attempt to make themselves American, his parents spoke English at home, rather than Russian or Yiddish, but it was accented and ungrammatical. With the help of his older brother, who took elocution lessons, he learned to speak 'correct' English 'as if it were Latin or Sanskrit', eventually acquiring an accent 'so impeccable that no one actually spoke that way except other people from Brooklyn who wished to sound as if they weren't'.

At Columbia University, he was one of the 'meatballs', the Jewish, Irish or Italian kids who could not afford to live on campus. While the more privileged students enjoyed their leisure time, he washed dishes, waited tables, sorted mail, tutored classmates and undertook umpteen other types of menial work. Yet his cohort at Columbia became legendary for producing a stream of public intellectuals, most of them Jewish – among them Mortimer Adler, Meyer Schapiro and Lionel Trilling. One of the few gentiles among them, Whittaker Chambers, dubbed the circle *ernste Menschen* ('serious men'), whose ardour for learning he attributed to 'a struggle with a warping poverty impossible for those who have not glimpsed it to imagine'. Fadiman had ambitions to become an academic, and was clever enough to have succeeded, but prejudice stood in his way. At his graduation, the chairman of the English Department told him, 'We have room for only one Jew, and we have chosen Mr Trilling.'

One response to such unfairness was anger, to rail against injustice, and maybe to turn to communism, as several of the group (including Chambers) did. Another was to try to join the club, which is the route Fadiman took. He strove to imitate his WASP peers, becoming like them in speech, dress, habit and tastes. He worked ferociously hard to conceal the fact that he needed to work so hard. Wine was linked to this process of reinvention; to learn about wine was, as he often said, both civilized and civilizing. He preferred not to look back. 'It was better to lay down a dozen cases of first-growth Bordeaux, because each bottle brought him closer to something he could never reach, but in whose direction, like a plant bending toward the sun, he could still turn.'

Anne Fadiman writes tenderly and movingly about her father, yet her memoir never cloys; she remains clear-sighted about his failings even while she arouses our sympathy for him. And in her portrait of him, she evokes an entire era of American life, and draws out the differences between then and now.

She was the daughter of his second marriage, born when he was already 49. As a child she was self-conscious about her father, who was 'too smart, too square, too odd, and too old'. To her friends he seemed genial but fuddy-duddy. When she was 8 the family moved from Connecticut to Los Angeles. Her friends' fathers radiated West Coast informality; her own father preferred not just 'East Coast decorum' but what he called 'English good manners'. When the school's annual Father-Daughter picnic rolled around, she contrived to leave him at home, and tagged along instead with her cousin, whose father was 'younger, taller, more likely to acquit himself credibly in a volleyball game, and generally less embarrassing'. Only later did she realize how much she must have hurt him.

From about the age of 10 Anne and her brother were offered watered-down wine at mealtimes. 'I hated it but assumed that puberty would grant me a taste for Châteauneuf-du-Pape, along with a taste for French kissing and all the other things that ten-year-olds found disgusting but adults reportedly enjoyed.' It was not until she was in her late 40s that she finally admitted to herself that she would never love wine as her father had done.

Yet for all that, her father's love of wine was genuine. After his death she found among his effects a folder entitled 'Wine Memorabilia', including a list of wines from his own cellar served at a small private dinner to celebrate his forty-ninth birthday on 15 May 1953 (one of his guests was Alistair Cooke); an article he had written called 'Remembrance of Drinks Past'; and his cellar book, 'the most serious book he ever wrote, the most heartfelt, the most honest'. Browsing through this folder, she remembered her father more vividly than at any moment since his death. 'The folder seemed to glow with joy, as if the memory of my father's pleasure was so strong as to render it faintly radioactive.'

ADAM SISMAN is a writer, specializing in biography. His most recent book is *The Professor and the Parson: A Story of Desire, Deceit and Defrocking* (2019). You can also hear him discussing the art of biography on our podcast, Episode 6, 'Well-Written Lives'.

Anne Fadiman's *The Wine Lover's Daughter: A Memoir* (204pp) is now available in a limited and numbered cloth-bound edition of 2,000 copies (subscribers: UK & Eire £17, Overseas £19; non-subscribers: UK & Eire £18.50, Overseas £20.50). All prices include post and packing. Copies may be ordered by post (53 Hoxton Square, London N1 6PB), by phone (020 7033 0258) or via our website www.foxedquarterly.com.

On the Slime Line

FRANCES DONNELLY

Those of us who prize a good literary thriller well above the price of rubies play a game resembling Fantasy Football. In our version we argue as to who are the top five thriller writers, then brood over which is their best book. For myself, the American author Martin Cruz Smith has never moved out of the top five, and his superlative *Polar Star* (1989), a story of murder and espionage on a Soviet fish-processing ship in the Bering Sea, is the book I most revisit.

'Why not *Gorky Park*?' fellow players often ask me. That was, of course, Cruz Smith's first, bestselling novel. But his second book, in addition to being very funny, contains writing almost worthy of Conrad himself. He brilliantly evokes the power and terror of the sea and the way it shapes the character of those who work in peril on it. As in *Gorky Park* the central actor is Arkady Renko, a former Moscow police inspector, a good man in a difficult place. But *Polar Star* is not a sequel. It's another magnificent stand-alone thriller.

The actual *Polar Star* is a vast, battered factory ship of the Soviet Far Eastern Fleet, ploughing its way from Siberia to Alaska, processing fish caught by four attendant American trawlers. But in crime-fiction terms it's a classic set-up: a closed community with discomfort and unease running at peak levels for four months at a time. Many of its crew are either on the run or, in Soviet speak, 'politically unreliable'. Renko is both.

In *Gorky Park* Renko was trying to prevent the illegal export of

Martin Cruz Smith, *Polar Star* (1989)
Simon & Schuster · Pb · 464pp · £16.99 · ISBN 9781471131097

live Russian sables. It ended badly – he foiled the plot but en route killed the Public Prosecutor and then set the animals free. For three years he's been hiding in Siberia. Its immense landmass and paralysing January temperature of minus 25 degrees means that even the Moscow police have (temporarily) lost interest in Renko. But a wise man keeps changing jobs. Renko's latest employment is on the slime line of the *Polar Star*. And it's an occupation quite as awful as it sounds.

On the slime line you end every shift with a face – skin, eyelashes, eyebrows – coated in a fine mist of blood, fish scales and fish guts. Renko and his cohorts work in pairs on either side of a conveyor belt of fish, sawing, gutting, beheading and filleting. If you're lucky you end your shift only frozen and numb. If you're unlucky, the saws can remove fingers as well. Someone with a strong stomach then has to search through the discarded fish heads for the missing digit so it can be sewn on again. In this frozen hell Renko should have been safe. That is until, in the novel's amazingly visceral opening scene, a trawl net crammed with fish reveals another, more sinister catch.

'Like a beast, the net came streaming up the ramp on to the trawl deck, water hissing from the net's plastic hair. Smaller fish fell free. Starfish dropped like stones.' Manoeuvring this colossal load with an almost balletic skill is the trawl master, Karp Korobetz, the *Polar Star*'s model employee, a barrel-chested, gold-toothed, heavily tattooed monolith, the Soviet worker at his most puissant. But Korobetz spots something that shouldn't be in the net and slices it open. 'Out of the net spilled a flood of silver pollock, a whole school dredged up like silver coins. And a girl. She slid with them, loose limbed like a swimmer, as the fish poured from the net.'

It is Zina Patiashvelli, a worker on the *Polar Star*, who formerly served food in the workers' mess.

Faced with this terrifying irregularity, the ship's political officer, Volovoi, a humourless jobsworth, can't believe his luck that there is a Moscow policeman on the slime line. Renko can't believe his bad luck at being that policeman. Volovoi is anxious that Renko should 'investigate' Zina's death, in other words tidy it away. How about food poisoning? She worked in the galley, after all.

Unfortunately, after a very rudimentary examination, Renko discovers Zina died of a blow to the head. She was thrown overboard, with a knife wound to the stomach to make sure she sank to the sea floor, where her corpse was colonized by slime eels. Don't ask about the slime eels. Then, a day later and against all the odds, the trawl net swept her up with the fish and back on to the *Polar Star*.

Keen-eyed readers will already be wondering why, at the height of the Soviet era, Russian and American boats are working together. The answer is of course perestroika, or 'thinking in new ways', Gorbachev's desperate last-ditch attempt at modernizing the ailing Soviet economy. America supplies the trawlers and keeps the money from the catch. Russia keeps the fish. But the presence of the Americans, as Renko gradually discovers, has created other possibilities – including smuggling and defection.

A bogus explanation for Zina's death is hastily cobbled together but Renko, to his own surprise, refuses to sign it off. For three years he's lived a life without any goal but survival. Against all the odds, Zina's body was resurrected from the sea. Is some kind of resurrection possible for him too? An exasperated captain gives him two days to try to find the real killer.

The characters who people this book are vividly drawn, none more touchingly than the assistant Renko choses from the slime line to help him solve Zina's murder. Transparently honest, immensely dignified and an inveterate reader of a field of literature known as 'tractor romances', Natasha Chaikovskaya is described as a woman with the soul of Carmen trapped inside the body of a Soviet shotputter. But he chooses well – twice she saves Renko's life, and she helps him to untangle the threads that led to Zina's death.

Part of my deep admiration for Cruz Smith is informed by knowledge of his long journeyman apprenticeship as a writer. Bill Smith, as he is known in his family, had written nineteen books under eight pseudonyms – spy stories, Westerns, science fiction plus tales of a gypsy art dealer – before he hit gold with *Gorky Park*. Not that that book's genesis was remotely straightforward. The publishers wanted a story about an American cop who goes to Moscow to solve a crime. Smith agreed, then found that Arkady Renko, a Moscow detective, strode out of his subconscious and insisted on taking centre stage. The New York cop was consigned to a minor role. The book was duly written but not liked. Over the next eight years, the publishers kept asking: why isn't the American the hero? They wouldn't publish it but they wouldn't let him buy it back either. What gave that refusal scene its special piquancy was that his editor, during the interview, actually cut his own toenails, having removed his shoes and socks shortly after Cruz Smith arrived. Then a new management with better hygiene habits took over and agreed to let him buy it back. Whereupon Cruz Smith sold it, almost immediately, for a million dollars. Truly a story to gladden the heart.

But what I love most about Martin Cruz Smith is clearly illustrated by his reflection about that enforced standoff. Far from being bitter, he commented: 'That long hiatus of writing and rewriting that book did me a huge favor. I had always had something to say, but by the time I actually finished it, I was better equipped to say it.' A typically generous summing up by a wonderfully gifted and generous writer.

FRANCES DONNELLY lives on the Norfolk/Suffolk border, and is still in search of a rescue dog. Ideally small, easy-going with GSOH essential.

The Elephant Man in the Room

DANIEL CREAMER

It would appear that many people love 'clinical writing', a distinct genre that embraces doctors, diseases and patients. As a medic I tend to avoid this territory. Stories about medical practice lean either to the sententious (e.g. A. J. Cronin's *The Citadel*) or the facetious (Richard Gordon's *Doctor in the House*), while the current big sellers favour medical heroics in war zones or harrowing tales from that other front-line of combat, the NHS. Also, I don't much care for the doctors who appear in novels. Who would employ Dr Tertius Lydgate, the idealistic young physician in *Middlemarch*, whose professional ambitions are so easily thwarted by the pretty, but shallow, Rosamund Vincy? And what about Dr Zhivago? Poet, lover and counter-revolutionary but, let's face it, not much of a physician.

Having said all that, and invoking the exception that proves the rule, I am a fan of one medical book, *The Elephant Man and Other Reminiscences*, which was written by a splendid Victorian surgeon called Frederick Treves. Published in 1923, the year Treves died, it is a series of vignettes about curious patients and his surgical practice during the last decades of the nineteenth century. It includes, of course, the remarkable story of Joseph Merrick, the Elephant Man, and how Treves rescued this terribly deformed man and helped him to health and happiness. But there are eleven other wonderful stories in this volume, the whole collection forming a gloriously odd anthology of medical Victoriana.

Frederick Treves, *The Elephant Man and Other Reminiscences* (1923), is out of print, but we can obtain second-hand copies.

In the 1880s Treves was a surgeon working at the London Hospital in Whitechapel (now the Royal London Hospital) and specializing in the new field of abdominal surgery which, at the time, was moving from being universally lethal to just highly dangerous. In 1888 he performed the first appendectomy in England and was thereafter in demand as the country's leading abdominal surgeon. His surgical skill was needed in June 1902 when King Edward VII developed acute appendicitis two days before his coronation. The King was utterly opposed to an operation. Treves was insistent, famously stating that if he was forbidden to operate there would be a royal funeral, not a coronation. The operation was duly performed on a table in the Music Room at Buckingham Palace and the following day Edward was well enough to sit up in bed and smoke a cigar. A grateful monarch elevated Treves to the Baronetcy.

Treves wrote throughout his professional life, his early publications being papers in medical journals and surgical textbooks. In 1900 he published *The Tale of a Field Hospital*, an account of his experiences as a combat surgeon in South Africa during the Boer War. This was hugely successful and spurred Treves to the ultimate act of surgical bravery: he retired. Treves maintained that a surgeon's technical dexterity deteriorates after the age of 50, a truism which is sadly as ignored today as it was back then.

Once he had given up his surgical practice he travelled the globe and wrote a series of books based on his adventures. The most charming (but least glamorous) is his *Highways and Byways of Dorset*, in which he documented the villages, people and customs of his native county following a series of epic bicycle journeys. In recognition of this devotion to all things Dorset he was elected the first president of the Society of Dorset Men (the second being his great friend Thomas Hardy).

While Treves's travel books have long since been forgotten, *The Elephant Man and Other Reminiscences* continues to fascinate. It is a fabulous piece of medical writing in which doctors, patients and the practice of medicine are blended to produce a book rich in colour and texture.

> What a strange company they are, these old patients who crowd into the surgeon's memory after a lifetime of busy practice. There they stand, a confused, impersonal assembly, so illusive and indistinct as to be little more than shadows . . . However among the phantoms of the casebook are some who are remembered with a completeness which appears never to have grown dim.

Although Treves uses the clinical casebook format, the contingency of medical practice is offset by his psychological acuity. His stories are about patients as people: what interests him is the person behind the illness and the curious way diseases and disorders shape and misshape our lives. One story, 'A Case of Nerves', is recounted by the patient, a young married woman who is suffering from pathological anxiety. She talks about her morbid fears and in recording them Treves delivers a masterclass in the psychiatric and physical symptoms of depression. 'The Idol with Hands of Clay' is a cautionary tale of an inexperienced but ambitious surgeon who is foolishly persuaded to operate on his young wife . . . To those of us who have been present at an operation which goes wrong, the nightmarish panic that follows is almost too horrible to bear.

However, the gem in the collection is of course 'The Elephant Man', the story by which Treves achieved fame beyond medical circles. It is the extraordinary tale – all entirely true – of Joseph Merrick, a young man hideously disfigured by congenital abnormalities, who at the time we first meet him is being exhibited as a freak in a travelling show. Most of us will know the story from the 1980 film in which Anthony Hopkins plays Treves, and John Hurt, unrecognizable in prosthetic make-up, is Joseph Merrick. Treves's account begins in 1884 when the Elephant Man was being held captive by his 'impresario' in a deserted shop opposite the London Hospital. Frederick Treves managed to secure a private viewing:

The showman pulled back the curtain and revealed a bent figure crouching on a stool and covered by a brown blanket . . .
The most striking feature about him was his enormous and
misshapen head. From the brow there projected a huge bony
mass like a loaf, while from the back of the head hung a bag of
spongy, fungous-looking skin, the surface of which was compar-
able to a cauliflower . . . The osseous growth on the forehead
almost occluded one eye . . . From the upper jaw there projected another mass of bone. It protruded from the mouth like
a pink stump, turning the upper lip inside out and making of
the mouth a mere slobbering aperture.

Poor Merrick – his deformities were horrifying, his existence
unspeakably degrading. Following this first encounter Treves's initial
act was to spirit Merrick into the hospital for a clinical examination
of his anatomical abnormalities, subsequently published in the *British
Medical Journal*. Merrick was then released back to the 'impresario'
and to his life on the road. Two years later, however, in Brussels,
he was abandoned by his tormentor and placed on a boat back to
London. He finally reached Liverpool Street station where, starved
and mute, he was found in a state of collapse. Treves's card was among
his possessions and so he was duly shepherded to the London
Hospital and into Treves's custody.

Treves arranged for Merrick to be admitted to a small room overlooking the yard where the hospital beds were stored, known as
Bedstead Square. This room became his home for the rest of his life.
Once he was installed and secure in the hospital's care, Treves
befriended him and, beneath the disfigurements, discovered an in-
telligent, affectionate man. The rehabilitation of Joseph Merrick is
chronicled with wonder and tenderness, a transformation which
is echoed in Treves's own increasing astonishment as his patient is
revealed to be a man supremely receptive to the beauty of life.

Despite being abandoned as an infant, Merrick revered the memory of his mother and was convinced of her beauty. He took to reading romantic novels and, in his imagination, cherished an emotional and idealized devotion to women. Alas the hospital nurses were unable to hide their revulsion and so Treves, recognizing the importance of feminine company, asked a young widow friend to pay Merrick a visit.

> The effect upon poor Merrick was not quite what I had expected. As he let go her hand he bent his head on his knees and sobbed until I thought he would never cease. The interview was over. He told me afterwards that this was the first woman who had ever smiled at him, and the first woman, in the whole of his life, who had shaken hands with him.

Word spread of this remarkable young man and soon society people, including Princess Alexandra, began to visit Merrick in his room overlooking Bedstead Square. Treves documented his delight in this extraordinary transformation. 'Merrick, I may say, was now one of the most contented creatures I have chanced to meet. More than once he said to me: "I am happy every hour of the day."' Treves was a devoted friend to Merrick and ensured that all was done to enrich his existence and mitigate the horrors of his previous life. But his health was fragile and in 1890 Merrick died from asphyxia at the age of 27. Treves, who performed the autopsy, suggested that his airway had been occluded by the weight of his head as he lay flat, a sleeping posture incompatible with his deformities.

> He often said to me that he wished he could lie down to sleep 'like other people'. I think on this last night he must, with some determination, have made the experiment. The pillow was soft. And the head, when placed on it, must have fallen backwards and caused a dislocation of the neck.

Following his death Merrick's skeleton was displayed in the hospital's museum until, in the 1980s, a group of medical students from

St Bartholomew's Hospital abducted him. Happily, Merrick was repatriated and on his return to the London his bones were carefully stored in the hospital's pathology department where they remain.

The hero of 'The Elephant Man', however, is not Treves or Joseph Merrick. It is the London Hospital. If there is a moral to this fable (a true fable) it is that in a civilized society there are institutions of refuge which exist to protect vulnerable people. The London Hospital has a long history of caring for East Enders, people who live in a socially disadvantaged part of the metropolis. In 1886 the hospital found a way to house Merrick and to nurture him. It is, I suppose, a version of *The Hunchback of Notre Dame*; the outcast who finds sanctuary in one of the city's charitable foundations. I find this thought both reassuring and deeply moving.

DANIEL CREAMER is a dermatologist at King's College Hospital, London. During his training he worked at St Thomas's, Guy's, St Mary's and St George's hospitals in London, but never at the London Hospital.

Death and the Duchess

LAURIE GRAHAM

I'm not usually tempted by biographies of royals, living or not long dead. They tend to be written in deferential tones and I prefer something neutral or, better yet, something with teeth. However, twenty years ago, when I was preparing to write my novel *Gone with the Windsors*, I read a huge number of books about the Duke and Duchess. Panegyrics, hatchet jobs, you name it. Hugo Vickers's *Behind Closed Doors* had yet to be published. When it came out in 2011, I felt compelled to read it. Vickers had no axe to grind. He hadn't known the Windsors. Could he deliver the sharp-eyed skinny?

In case you're too young to remember, here is the short version of 'The Love Story of the Century'. Once upon a time a popular English prince, with more charm than brains, fell in love with a sassy American divorcée who didn't give a fig for stuffy royal protocol. They ran away to distant shores and lived controversially ever after.

In the 1930s, when Edward VIII abdicated and married Wallis Simpson, it was a very big deal indeed. The notoriety that engulfed them seems rather overblown today. Yes, he gave up the Throne, but his brother made a perfectly good and some would say better King. Yes, the Windsors flirted with Nazism, but in the Thirties so did more Brits than is now comfortable to remember.

The abdication shock aside, opinions of the Windsors varied. They were a breath of fresh air. They were grotesque freeloaders. He was a modern man, in tune with the average Joe in the street. No, he was

Hugo Vickers, *Behind Closed Doors* (2011)
Arrow · Pb · 480pp · £12.99 · ISBN 9780099547228

a besotted fool, a rabbit beguiled by a ferret. Wallis was *le dernier mot* in Dior-clad elegance – a capital crime among the cardigan-wearers of upper-crust England. She was a sexually magnetic siren. No, she was a bloke in drag. Were they living proof that love conquers all or just a pair of ill-matched gadflies making the best of a bad job?

Vickers's book, oddly, is arranged back-to-front. Part 2 is a familiar spin through the Duke and Duchess's back stories. Society names drop so thick and fast you may wish to wear a hard hat. But the meat of the matter, an account of the Windsors' twilight years, is served first, and what a gruesome dish it is.

Hugo Vickers never actually met either of them, though he was occasionally under the same roof. In 1972 he was sent to Paris by *Burke's Peerage* to interview the Duke for a proposed reference book. He arrived too late. At the house in the Bois de Boulogne the Duke was already close to death, closeted upstairs with nurses. Downstairs, life went grimly on. The Duchess's secretary was busy making couturier appointments and searching for a spare man for an imminent dinner party. What a pity Vickers felt too shy to offer himself.

It was a missed opportunity, but he recovered his courage sufficiently to wangle his way into the Duke's funeral, albeit assisting behind the scenes, and so was able to launch a long association with senior members of the Windsors' staff. That is our gain. If you want to know what really goes on, enquire below stairs.

Friends of the Duchess claimed she was already showing signs of frailty and confusion, though apparently not at the post-funeral lunch. When asked by Prince Philip if she planned to return to America she replied, 'I won't be coming here, if that's what you're worried about.' Nice return of serve.

At that point in her life two worries preoccupied her. First, she understood the social Siberia widows can face. She herself abhorred 'odds' at her table and had dropped a few widows in her time. Second, she feared poverty. The Duke had left his affairs in order and the Swiss bank account was in good health, but imminent penury is a common worry among the elderly. Enter, stage left, Suzanne Blum, a formidable Paris lawyer, who did nothing to reassure the Duchess.

How Mâitre Blum ever got her foot so firmly in the door is a mystery. The Windsors already had a perfectly good British lawyer. But they had been domiciled in France for many years and exempt from paying those pesky taxes. Mâitre Blum saw her opportunity and stepped in, to warn and advise. What if the French government reviewed the peppercorn rent the Duchess was paying, or even evicted her? What if they raided her widow's mite for back taxes? This was the spectre Mâitre Blum raised to alarm the Duchess and win control over her. She said she did it in the name of friendship. Others saw it as undue influence but still allowed it to continue. Georges, the major-domo, listener at doors and counter of spoons, did nothing. Sydney, valet and pug-walker general, turned a blind eye. Lord Mountbatten tried to raise the alarm, but Blum outflanked him. The Duchess, increasingly frail, subsisting on vodka and not much else, seemed too weak to send her packing. She was convinced she was down to her last *sou*. Perhaps, also, she was intimidated by a woman who looked like a butch version of her late mother-in-law, Queen Mary.

While the Duke lived, Wallis had had a purpose in life: to keep the Windsor show on the road. After his death, that role disappeared. For a year or two she tried to keep up appearances, popping into Chanel, tottering into Maxim's to dine on lettuce leaves. Then she faded from the social scene. She was sick, insomniac, terrified of break-ins. She took to her bed. And with the Duchess safely tucked away upstairs, things started to go missing. Paintings, porcelain, antiques. Hundreds of items were generously donated to Versailles, the Louvre and the Musée de Sèvres. Some might find it suspicious that soon after these donations were made, Mâitre Blum was promoted to a higher degree of the Légion d'honneur.

The Duchess survived the Duke by fourteen wretched years. She lay in her bed, cut off from friends who were told she was too ill to receive visitors, deprived of her beloved dogs which were deemed too germ-ridden to enter her room, and apparently oblivious of the fire sale going on downstairs. There was a mountain of stuff to dispose of. The gilt epergnes, the jade doodahs and gold snuff boxes. And whatever became of the Fabergé hippo?

Someone, probably the Duke's former private secretary, sent an SOS to Buckingham Palace: the Duchess is alone in the world and dying. There was no reply. The unofficial policy, directed by the Queen Mother, was to maintain a polite distance, and with Mountbatten's death in 1979, the Duchess lost her only royal advocate.

Mâitre Blum's final move was to wrest Power of Attorney from the Duchess's secretary, something she achieved like a chess grand master. Financial papers were burned, staff were let go, locks were changed. Vickers logs the chilling steps that left the Duchess powerless and trapped in a body that didn't know how to die.

When death did come, in 1986, many were surprised to discover that she'd been alive all those years, but one man who had kept track was Mohamed Al-Fayed. He already had his eye on the house and saw its potential as a museum and permanent memorial. The Royal Family might have treated the Windsors with disdain, but he would redress that wrong. There was something apposite about Al-Fayed's interest. Wallis's taste in décor had once been characterized as 'very Harrods'. Ouch.

The Windsors tended to bring out the killer wasp in commentators. When she was still Mrs Simpson, Wallis had been dismissed as 'an ambitious housewife, clambering on to the foothills of London society'. Later, Cecil Beaton described her as 'a brawny bullock in sapphire blue velvet'. And here's Edith Wharton, commenting on the Duke's stay at a Rothschild castle in Austria while he waited for Wallis's decree absolute: 'Fiction writers had better go out of business if King Edward VIII is taking refuge with the ex-wife of a Brooklyn dentist.' It's hard to know which is the more toe-curling: that snobbish sketch of Baroness Rothschild or the reports that the Duke, when he lodged with her, was a complaining, ungrateful guest.

The Duchess's death wasn't the end of the story. Mohamed Al-Fayed bought the lease on the house and proceeded to redecorate, reportedly with some touches that might have been over the top even for the Duchess. Hard to believe. Her taste for faux marble and knock-off Louis Quinze was once judged 'ghastly' by some snooty arbiter of style. And as for all those china pugs, well . . .

Despite the years of quiet decluttering by Mâitre Blum, there remained a quantity of Windsoriana to sell, notably Wallis's considerable collection of jewels. When the vault was opened and its contents compared with the official inventory, some items were already missing. Light-fingered friends are apparently a cross the ostentatiously wealthy have to bear. The major pieces were auctioned in Geneva and realized a stunning £31 million. The name of the beneficiary of these proceeds came as a surprise to everyone who had known the Duchess. The Louis Pasteur Institute got the lot.

The Pasteur Institute was an esteemed and worthy legatee, but not one in which the Duchess had ever expressed the slightest interest. When questioned, Mâitre Blum conceded that the bequest had been her suggestion but that the Duchess had been in full agreement. Vickers, who regarded Suzanne Blum as Satan in tweeds, tells us that no written evidence was ever produced to prove that the Duchess, confused, mute and too arthritic to hold a pen, had signed anything. And he reminds us that soon after the legacy was paid to the Institute, Mâitre Blum rose still further in the Légion d'honneur. But of course, this too may have been entirely coincidental.

Vickers delivers. He neither fawns nor condemns. He simply reports, with an eye for the telling detail and a nose for the smell of a rat, what he observed. Read it and you can't help but feel pity for the Duchess at the end of her long life.

LAURIE GRAHAM is a novelist and journalist. She would have loved to see what use the Windsors might have made of social media had they been alive today.

'Hold on tight . . . and believe'

LINDA LEATHERBARROW

As I walked through the quiet twilight streets of the little Scottish fishing town in which I live, I unexpectedly came across two figures lounging on a pair of deckchairs. One was dressed in dark trousers, a red tartan jacket and matching tam-o'-shanter, while the other wore a silver sequined dress and an elaborate blonde wig. Although they were both strangely motionless, it was only when I got much closer that I realized these were not actually living people. They were dressed-up plastic skeletons, their gaping mouths laughing, their bony fingers pointing at me. How macabre, I thought, how gruesome. How very Stephen King.

Here I must confess that I'd never read any of King's fiction. Although more than 350 million copies of his novels have been sold, something about the way in which they were marketed had always put me off and I'd dismissed him as a writer of sensationalist horror. I'd forgotten that horror was a genre I'd happily devoured as a teenager, mostly in bed, under the blankets, by torchlight. Vampires, werewolves, ghosts and ghouls, in all the classic novels: Mary Shelley's *Frankenstein*, Bram Stoker's *Dracula* and H. P. Lovecraft's *The Thing Without a Name*. Perhaps now, I thought, over half a century later, it was time to abandon my preconceptions and give Stephen King a try.

My local bookshop offered a wide range of his work and I soon discovered that King didn't just write horror. He also wrote thrillers, science fiction, fantasy, as well as books about the supernatural. Born

Stephen King, *Nightmares & Dreamscapes* (1993)
Hodder · Pb · 992pp · £10.99 · ISBN 9781444723182

in Portland, Maine, in 1947, he began writing while he was still at school and sold the stories to friends. His first officially published story, 'I Was a Teenage Grave Robber', was serialized in four issues of *Comics Review* in 1965. Now, in addition to his fifty-eight novels, there are five books of non-fiction, seven novellas and over two hundred stories published in eleven collections. Intrigued, I chose his third collection, *Nightmares & Dreamscapes*, which contains twenty stories and was published in 1993.

In his Introduction, King explains that it was a compilation of amazing facts and curiosities, called *Ripley's Believe It or Not*, that first got his imagination going and allowed him to see 'how fine the line between the fabulous and the humdrum could sometimes be'. As a child, when it was raining or he had no homework, he liked to curl up with *Ripley's* and read its extraordinary claims: for example, that there were actual giants (one man over eight feet tall) and actual elves (a woman barely eleven inches). Apparently, *Ripley's* also claimed that there were MONSTERS TOO HORRIBLE TO DESCRIBE but then went on to do so. Describing his own stories, King says:

> Each contains something I believed for a while and I know that some of these things – the finger pointing out of the drain, the man-eating toads, the hungry teeth – are a little frightening, but I think we'll be all right if we go together . . . All you have to do is hold on tight . . . and *believe*.

Although he is an exceptionally inventive writer, his lucid story-telling makes belief surprisingly easy. The first story I read was 'The Night Flier' in which Richard Dees, a reporter who writes for the tabloid *Inside View*, has been asked by his editor to track down a man believed by their readers to be a vampire. There have already been two murders at a small local airport in Maryland and, knowing that the right picture on the front page could produce a much-needed circulation boost, Dees flies off to the airport, armed only with his camera and a large degree of scepticism.

It's the details and descriptions that help to make this story so realistic and plausible. Using familiar brands and model numbers, King sets up the humdrum normality that fills his characters' lives. He describes the General Aviation Terminal with its two criss-crossing runways, one tarred and one dirt, and tells us that Dees, who uses an old Nikon camera bought in a Toledo hockshop when he was 17, was given landing clearance at 7.45 p.m., less than forty minutes before official sundown. Vampires, of course, only come out at night, but this one has a private pilot's licence and flies a Cessna Skymaster 337 with red piping and the number NIOIEL on the tail.

Dees believed the Night Flier was a real vampire about as much as he believed it was the Tooth Fairy who had put all those quarters under his pillow when he was a kid, but if the guy thought he was a vampire – and this guy, Dees was convinced, really did – that would probably be enough to make him conform to the rules.

Dees is hoping for a photograph of the man dressed to kill, the rules in this case being black tuxedo pants and a bat-wing cloak. But King, who also understands the importance of conforming to the rules, knows that if you give your readers a fake vampire you will only disappoint. So, in the climax at the airport, as Dees is washing his hands in the basement men's room, he senses somebody close by and looks in the mirror, but there's nobody there. Too late, he remembers that real vampires have no reflection. 'Open your camera,' demands an ageless voice.

A master of his craft, King never tries to explain the situation in which his characters find themselves; he simply records the actions that arise from it. Although his descriptions are always apt and evocative, he largely avoids distracting metaphors or poetic imagery. His plain, down-to-earth voice appears to tell it as it is, leading the reader on, from the urgent normality of the set-up to the surprising climax.

Most of the stories are set in the USA – several in Maine, where King grew up, another in Nevada, one in front of the First Mercantile Bank of Boston, and one in a grand old hotel in New York. There is even a little town in Oregon, inhabited by ghosts from the pop world: Janis Joplin, Rick Nelson, Roy Orbison and Buddy Holly. However, two stories are set in London, one close to where I used to live. In 'Crouch End', King describes the area around Tottenham Lane police station as a place where 'more strange things happen than anywhere else in London'. Not quite as I remember it.

The other, 'The Doctor's Case', begins at 221b Baker Street and is a 'new' Sherlock Holmes mystery. At first, I wasn't sure if King with his distinctly American voice would be able to pull this off, but he succeeds triumphantly. His familiar narrator, Dr Watson, now in his ninth decade, has a distinctly British voice, very Arthur Conan Doyle. Also, for the first time – and rather delightfully, I thought – it's Dr Watson who actually solves the case.

While most of the stories in this collection could be categorized as horror, fantasy or suspense, 'My Pretty Pony' is a touching and beautifully written 'instruction' about the passage of time. Here we have a grandfather engaged in a serious conversation with his grandson. The old man, who seemed to the boy 'older than God, which probably meant about seventy-two', takes a tarnished silver watch out of his pocket, gives it to the boy and tells him he may keep it. 'You ain't gonna drop it, and if you did you probably wouldn't stop it,' his grandfather said, but the boy is old enough to know that, one day, both watches and people *do* stop. However, it's only much later that he realizes, when his grandfather was talking about his 'ticka', he was actually talking about his heart. Time is the pretty pony, a wicked beast, always speeding up as we get older.

In the Notes to the collection, King explains that this story was originally a flashback in a novel which his alter-ego, Richard Bachman, was struggling to complete. 'A bad piece of work born in an unhappy time,' he writes. Although King scrapped the novel, fortunately he saved the flashback. It was, he says, 'like finding a rose growing in a junkheap'.

Also in the Notes, King describes an encounter with a reader who told him that she preferred to skip Notes. 'I'm one of those people who don't want to know how the magician does his tricks,' she said. King explains that he is not a magician and these are not tricks. However, he does believe there is a certain magic involved in writing fiction, not in the text, but at that moment when a story pops into a writer's head, often just a fragment but sometimes a whole story.

When King was invited to take part in a panel discussion, held in a bookshop in Manhattan, he was asked if he could recall anything in his childhood that was particularly terrible. In response he repeated an anecdote his mother had told him. Apparently, when he was only 4, he'd gone off to play at a friend's house – a house close to a railway line – and when he came back, he was as pale as a ghost and wouldn't speak for the rest of the day. 'It turned out that the kid I'd been play-ing with had been run over by a freight train.' King claimed to have no actual memory of the event, but then another member of the panel, a psychiatrist, chipped in. 'You've been writing about it ever since,' she said.

I believe it's true that writing about difficult events or turning them into stories may often help a writer cope. Perhaps reading hor-ror stories may also help the reader to re-evaluate their worst fears. I hope King's readers will not just be gripped and scared but will also experience a little cathartic comfort.

LINDA LEATHERBARROW's prize-winning and broadcast short stories are published in her collections *Essential Kit* and *Funny Things Families*.

Contemplating Eternity

MARIANNE FISHER

Although I want to tell you about a poem, let us begin with objects. I would like you to come with me first to Birmingham, to visit the Staffordshire Hoard. These rich and intricately worked treasures, most of which were once decorations for weapons, conjure images of kings and warriors in the Dark Ages: Anglo-Saxon noblemen, proud and brave, the gold and garnets on their war gear flashing in the light of the sixth-century sun. The few objects that are not overtly martial are religious, and these show us how Christianity and paganism overlapped in England at this time: there are Christian crosses in the hoard, but they are decorated with the interlaced plants and animals characteristic of the pagan Germanic peoples. Perhaps most of all, though, the Staffordshire Hoard makes one think of passing, inheritance and decline. Some of the objects are decorated with re-used Roman glass, a reminder both of Roman technology and of Rome's fall; more poignantly still, the majority of the items were systematically dismantled or broken up before they were buried, the precious metals and stones separated from the iron, wood, bone and cloth they once adorned. There must have been a reason for this, but that reason is lost, and those who understood it have been dust for centuries.

Let us now go west, across the Irish Sea to Dublin, to see the Book of Kells. The legend, attested since 1007, is that this lavish gospel book was written in the hand of St Columba himself (the Irish monk who founded the Christian community on Iona, and died in

---

David Jones, *The Anathemata* (1952)
Faber · Pb · 272pp · £20 · ISBN 9780571259793

AD 597), though it is now thought to date from sometime between the late seventh and mid-ninth centuries. Created either on Iona or in Ireland itself, the Book of Kells is Celtic and sacred whereas the Staffordshire Hoard is Anglo-Saxon and martial; instead of Dark Age action, weapons, kings and warriors, here we have contemplation, text, monks and, in the first full-page illustration, the Virgin and Child. But the manuscript shares to some degree the hybrid nature of the hoard: the gospel text is in Latin, the illustrations have affinities with Greek and Coptic iconography, and much of the other decoration is, again, in the interlaced, knotted style inherited from pagan culture. Admiring the Book of Kells, however, is a very different experience from admiring the Staffordshire Hoard, for, while the treasure is elegiac, the manuscript is an intrinsically joyous and hopeful object. Its texts are those of the Good News, its essence faith in salvation, its purpose to redeem humankind from linear time and decline, and find us a home in eternity.

For our last stops en route to the poem, we shall return to Great Britain and visit Cardiff and London (or Google) to look at two of David Jones's paintings: *Trystan ac Essyllt* (1962, National Museum of Wales) and *Aphrodite in Aulis* (1941, Tate). These are beautiful, complex pictures that repay prolonged viewing, the former illustrating a scene from the Arthurian legend, which Jones loved deeply; the latter a female nude invoking many of the themes we have touched on already. They also share a characteristic style that makes visible the style of the poem: fluid, shifting, transparent, the layers overlapping and bleeding together to give an effect rather like looking through running water or mist. It is magical, stimulating and at times slightly unsettling.

Why begin like this? Partly because David Jones was, besides being a poet, also a soldier, devout Catholic, artist, engraver, Londoner and Welshman; and partly because these objects have introduced ideas, themes and techniques that run through his great poem. *The Anathemata*, in that allusive, layered, overlapping style of the paintings, embraces the Christian and the pagan, the sacred and the profane, elegy and praise, the passing and the circularity of time, the nobility and the transience of human endeavour. It is, in essence, an extended love song to Britain and the West, and to the culture and civilization they have inherited from Greece and Rome.

In 200-odd pages of verse, prose, image and inscription, the poem explores, and muses on, the development of humankind from its pre-human ancestors; the formation of Europe, both geological and cultural; the nature of human beings as creatures who make things; and, key to it all, faith and the Christian mysteries. Another central theme is what scholars call *translatio* – the notion that knowledge and power drift ever westward, from Babylon to Greece, to Rome, to France and Britain (and, we might add, on to America and perhaps beyond, back round to China and India). This idea of passage provides much of the poem's imagery – ships and sea travel abound, successive waves of migration and immigration are registered in Britain's past, and the layers of history are laid down like rock strata, passing successively out of sight yet each underpinning the next, preserving the last, and all to some degree retrievable, none irredeemably lost.

The Anathemata is Jones's second long poem. The first, the war epic *In Parenthesis*, was published by Faber in 1937; *The Anathemata* followed in 1952. The word 'anathemata' (accent on the third syllable) means something like 'things set apart' – not in the sense of being made anathema, though the words are related, but, as Jones summarizes in the poem's preface, 'Things set up, lifted up, or in whatever manner made over to the gods.' That is clearly how he saw his poem, and, indeed, all his work as an artist. Though not in the least 'churchy', *The Anathemata* is, nevertheless, a kind of offering.

The poem is divided into eight parts, their titles indicating the ritualistic, mythical atmosphere of the whole. 'Rite and Fore-Time' meditates on the evolutionary origins of humankind and the geological formation of the European continent, and in doing so attempts to mesh pre-history with Christian time. Jones considers all the unknown multitudes – the first proto-human to walk erect, those who went naked in tropical climes and the fur-clad 'tundra wanderers' of the last Ice Age, he who killed the last mammoth, and the nameless artists who decorated the caves at Lascaux – and comes to the beautiful, moving conclusion that if Christ died to redeem humankind, that redemption must include all these too:

> (He would lose, not any one
>   from among them.
> Of all those given him
>   he would lose none.)
>
> . . .
>
> Upon all fore-times.
>   From before time
> his perpetual light
>   shines upon them.
>   Upon all at once
> upon each one
> whom he invites, bids, us to recall
> when we make the recalling of him
>   daily, at the Stone.

In the next section, 'Middle-Sea and Lear-Sea', we creep gradually forward in time until, in dancing, lyrical mode, we reach classical Greece:

> and the second Spring
> and a new wonder under heaven:
>   man-limb stirs
>   in the god-stones
> and the kouroi
>   are gay and stepping it
> but stanced solemn.

Moving quickly now, in space as well as time, we join a weathered old Athenian shipmaster and his crew as they sail out from a choppy Mediterranean into yet rougher waters, headed north towards a myth-wrapped Britain. Storm-tossed, wind-driven, the ship-boys longing for their Greek girls back home, the section ends in mystery with the vessel shrouded in mist somewhere off Cornwall.

'Angle-Land' picks up where the previous section left off, as the ship of culture noses its way around Britain's southern and eastern coasts, where Romanitas and more recent Germanic influences mingle on a bed of pre-Roman Britishness. This section contains one of my favourite passages, which illustrates Jones's playful use of language and skill with sound (he was adamant that *The Anathemata* should be read aloud), as our sailor travels:

> On past the low lands of the Holland that
> Welland winds to the Deepings north of the Soke
> past where Woden's gang is *gens Julia* for Wuffingas new to
> old Nene and up with the Lark
> past the south hams and the north tons . . .

You don't need to understand all the references to appreciate just how lovely these words are; indeed, the sense of understanding only partially, of seeing the meaning 'as if through a glass, darkly', is part of the poem's appeal (and if you prefer clarity, the Internet will soon provide it). The passage then slides off into thoughts on Nelson at Trafalgar, before the section ends in the Anglo-European waters of the North Sea.

By Section IV, 'Redriff', our seaman has berthed his ship in a timeless London, but she needs repair. His enquiries give rise to a lively monologue from Eb Bradshaw, shipwright, Jones's grandpa, in the great boasting tradition inherited from *Beowulf*. No, Mr Bradshaw will not hurry the job, will not botch his work to suit this impatient foreigner,

But
    tell him
tell him from me
    if he waits his turn an' damps down his Sicily sulphur, we'll
spokeshave those deadeyes for him as smooth as a *peach* of a cheek
    . . . he's got
till the Day o' Doom
to sail the bitter seas o' the world!

'The Lady of the Pool', Section V, is the heart of the poem and belongs to women. Though the title invokes Arthurian romance, we remain in London, our lady a Cockney lavender-seller and docklands harlot called Elen, who has learnt much from her seafaring backstreet loves and is, in fact, a powerful, atemporal, mother-lover figure, embodying not merely London, but also Roma, Amor (Aphrodite), Flora, Guinevere, Helen, Mary . . . 'What rogue's cant is this?' she sharply asks the one man who senses some of her significance, 'Whereas, inly,' she confesses, 'I for love languished.'

In the middle of Elen's monologue is *The Anathemata*'s core: a lyrical account of the Passion that touches, typically, on the Liturgy, *The Canterbury Tales*, *The Waste Land* and the nursery rhyme 'Sing a Song of Sixpence'. Once Elen has lapsed back into her flower-seller's cry, Section VI, 'Keel, Ram, Stauros', charts the fate of an archetypal tree in ship, battering ram and Cross. Next, 'Mabinog's Liturgy' picks up themes from 'Rite and Fore-Time', but now located in Britain and closer to us in time, running right up to the Nativity itself and the joyous Christmas solemnities in Dark Age Wales and a timeless Rome, where we join the celebrants at dawn in the church of St Anastasia on the Palatine Hill:

Keeping this most stella'd night
on Christmas Day in the Morning.
Then back to Mary Major to hear them tell of how that from
before all time Minerva is sprung from the head of Jove.

The final section is called 'Sherthursdaye and Venus Day', but here I must make a confession: though I first encountered *The Anathemata* over a decade ago, I have not yet read this last section. The poem's style, as you will have noticed, is allusive, the language peppered with snatches of Latin, Welsh, German and Cockney rhyming slang. Though the references are not obscure, and Jones helps the reader with notes, *The Anathemata* is a demanding read. Jones writes in the preface of how every word is intended to mean 'as much as it can be made to mean', and expresses his wish that the poem be read 'with deliberation . . . for what I have written will certainly lose half of what I intend, indeed, will fail altogether, unless the advice "with deliberation" be heeded'. Reading like this is stimulating, rewarding, but not for every day. Thus, the poem comes off my shelf at the beginning of Advent each year, and returns to it on Twelfth Night. (I reckon I'll get to the end in 2023.) In between, I do read 'with deliberation', following the references out into the *OED*, encyclopaedias and literature, going slowly, looping back, annotating and cross-referencing to the extent that my copy is beginning to resemble one of those medieval bibles in which the scholastic commentary threatens to swamp the Scripture. There is just so much meaning to discover.

Though I say the references are not obscure, there are certain texts that loom particularly large in Jones's mental landscape. Among them are the Mass and Liturgy, the medieval Welsh tales of *The Mabinogion*, Malory's *Le Morte D'Arthur* and the Greek and Norse myths. Another book that profoundly influenced his thought is Spengler's *The Decline of the West*, which argues that so-called Great Cultures rise and fall, and that contemporary Western culture is in its twilight having been at its most vital in the early Middle Ages. This sense of transience and fading gives *The Anathemata* an aching sadness, much like that one experiences when looking at the Staffordshire Hoard – a pervasive awareness that we are living late in time, in the 'ramshackle last phases'. Yet this sadness is balanced by

Christian hope – for the New Light of the Book of Kells shines on us just as it did on our prehistoric forebears – and by faith in the power of art, humankind's defining trait, to preserve, offer up and pass on. 'I have made a heap of all that I could find', Jones writes at the start of his preface, quoting the ninth-century British chronicler Nennius, who wrote in the hope that the precious cultural detritus so gathered might be handed on and kept alive. Well, *The Anathemata* is a marvellous heap, built with the devotion and skill of a master-maker, and I can only urge you to seek it out as part of your own cultural inheritance, and to enjoy it for yourself. Even if it does take you a decade.

MARIANNE FISHER is native to the border between England and Wales, and discovered David Jones while at university in Cardiff. She usually acts as midwife to other people's prose, but she likes to write her own occasionally too.

David Jones (1895–1974), *He Frees the Waters in Helyon*, wood engraving
© Trustees of the David Jones Estate/Bridgeman Images

Death by Chocolate

MARTIN EDWARDS

Five years ago, I visited Pablo Neruda's former home in Valparaíso, now a museum. La Sebastiana is perched on a hillside with marvellous views out over the Pacific. When I reached the poet's study at the top of the house, the audio tour commentary mentioned the 'thrillers' that he'd enjoyed, some of which were gathering dust on the lowest shelf of a bookcase. My lifelong fascination with detective stories made it inevitable that I would get down on hands and knees and explore the books to see if Neruda and I shared any tastes.

There were a couple of dozen paperbacks, including – to my delight – dog-eared green Penguins written by a favourite author of mine, Anthony Berkeley. At one time, Berkeley's name was spoken in the same breath as that of Agatha Christie, and he was her own favourite detective novelist. Jorge Luis Borges also admired him. A gifted innovator, Berkeley wrote some of the cleverest novels in the crime genre as well as some of the most deeply ironic. Yet over the past eighty years he has become almost completely forgotten.

I first came across his name as a schoolboy, when I was already hooked on detective fiction. I was a fan of the BBC anthology series *Detective* in which an adaptation of Berkeley's short story 'The

Anthony Berkeley, *The Poisoned Chocolates Case* (1929), is available in the British Library Crime Classics series: 224pp · Pb · £8.99 · ISBN 9780712356534. *The Silk Stocking Murders* (1928) is available in the Collins Crime Club series: 256pp · Pb · £8.99 · ISBN 9780008333898. *The Layton Court Mystery* (1925), *Before the Fact* (1932) written under the pseudonym Francis Iles, and *Trial and Error* (1937) are out of print.

Avenging Chance' was screened, starring John Carson as the suave detective Roger Sheringham. The twists and turns of the plot appealed to me and so I scoured the local library for more of Berkeley's books. With one exception, the witty and ingenious *Trial and Error* (1937), they were all unavailable. So began my quest to hunt down the rest of his novels and discover more about the secretive, elusive man who wrote them.

Berkeley, whose real name was Anthony Berkeley Cox, was educated at Sherborne and Oxford; he fought in the First World War and suffered long-term health problems as a result of being gassed. After the Armistice, he began to contribute skits to *Punch* before writing a detective novel, *The Layton Court Mystery*, which was published in 1925.

In person, Berkeley was like Jekyll and Hyde, capable of both exceptional generosity and cold cynicism and grudge-bearing. I've met his niece, who was extremely fond of him, and corresponded with his stepdaughter, who loathed him. Under the name Francis Iles, he pioneered the psychological crime novel (Hitchcock filmed *Before the Fact* (1932) as *Suspicion* but gave this macabre story a happy ending that the author detested), but solving the puzzles of his own personality would challenge any psychiatrist. He dedicated one of his novels, *The Silk Stocking Murders* (1928), 'To A. B. Cox, who very kindly wrote this book for me in his spare time' and went so far as to inscribe a copy to himself. Weird.

His dysfunctional personal life included two disastrous marriages, and he protected his privacy with fanatical zeal. His early novels were published anonymously, and he refused to allow his photograph to appear on Penguin editions of his books. After 1939, following an emotional collapse, he stopped writing crime novels altogether, although he continued to review new books (with great insight: he was one of the first to spot the excellence of authors such as P. D. James and Ruth Rendell) until his death in 1971.

Berkeley was a highly influential figure during the so-called

'Golden Age of detective fiction' between the two world wars. Golden Age detective fiction is often misunderstood as 'cosy' but is really better regarded as a reaction to tragedy and horror. After years of slaughter – and an influenza pandemic that claimed even more lives – people just wanted to have fun. They craved escapism, and detective novelists (including those, like Berkeley, who had been seriously wounded in the conflict) supplied it in the form of whodunnits that allowed readers to compete with a fictional detective in solving a labyrinthine murder case. The author was expected to 'play fair' and give adequate clues in the text before all was revealed by an omniscient sleuth.

But Berkeley was sceptical about the notion of the infallible detective in the mould of Sherlock Holmes. He understood a fundamental truth that, to this day, political and other media commentators (as well as many other people) routinely ignore: *a set of facts is often susceptible to more than one interpretation*. He also recognized that the appeal of a detective story – or any crime story – lies not so much in seeing conventional justice done (after all, the criminal escapes punishment in several of Holmes's most memorable cases) but in tackling uncertainties, even if in an unorthodox way.

Roger Sheringham, in some respects an ironic self-portrait, was conceived as an offensive character whose smug confidence in his own brilliance is often misplaced. Sometimes the 'twist' is that his ingenious theories fall apart, while the plodders of Scotland Yard get it right. Berkeley's culprits tend to be more sympathetically portrayed than their victims, and the crimes often resemble acts of altruism. In his universe, the randomness of Fate is everywhere apparent. Time and again, people get away with murder.

'The Avenging Chance' concerns murder by poisoned chocolates, a common device of the genre. For a character in a Golden Age story to consume chocolates sent by an anonymous benefactor was invariably fraught with danger. The unthinking glee with which greedy recipients gobbled down deadly chocs seems all the more astonishing given the real-life precedent for crimes of this kind. In 1922, Sir William Horwood, the Metropolitan Police Commissioner, had himself almost died after consuming a walnut whip laced with arsenic that had been sent to him by a deranged member of the public. Horwood had persuaded himself that the chocolates were a birthday present, which tells us all we need to know about his own detective skills.

Berkeley decided that the plot of 'The Avenging Chance' had further potential. He developed it into a full-length book and *The Poisoned Chocolates Case* hit the shelves in 1929, shortly after Berkeley had begun to host dinners with fellow detective novelists. In those days, long before the arrival of social media and literary festivals, most crime writers didn't know each other. Berkeley's idea was to assemble those he regarded as the leaders in the field and form his own social network. In 1930, he founded the Detection Club and invited G. K. Chesterton to become its first President. The Club flourishes to this day.

The idea of the Club was buzzing in Berkeley's mind as he wrote the novel. Chief Inspector Moresby of Scotland Yard puts the facts about the poisoned chocolates before the six members of the Crimes Circle, a sort of embryonic version of the Detection Club hosted by Sheringham.

The publisher's blurb for the first edition proclaimed:

This is a detective story on a new plan. Instead of one detective and half a dozen suspects, there are half a dozen detectives and each of them suspects only one person! . . . Roger conceives the idea of setting his Circle the problem which has baffled the police. Each member in turn supplies a different solution. Which is the correct one?

Never has a detective story so dazzlingly exposed the risks of reading too much into apparently straightforward evidence. Each time one of the amateur sleuths comes up with an answer to the problem of 'Who killed Joan Bendix?', their reasoning seems convincing. And then someone else examines the case and comes up with a fresh interpretation of events . . .

Berkeley's flair and inventiveness are highlighted when Sheringham proposes the same solution as in 'The Avenging Chance' – only for one of his colleagues to shoot it down. Even then, Berkeley isn't finished. In Golden Age detective fiction, typically the 'twist ending' involves the revelation that the least likely suspect is actually the culprit. Here, meek little Ambrose Chitterwick, who appears least likely to solve a crime and is the last to speak, comes up with the most compelling explanation.

This is whodunnit game-playing at its wittiest and most subversive. The book's subtitle, *An Academic Detective Story*, underlines the fact that Berkeley's focus is not on emotional engagement or in-depth characterization, but rather on the dizzying possibilities of plot. What is more, Berkeley's friend and Detection Club colleague Christianna Brand later came up with a *seventh* solution to his puzzle for an American reprint.

After the Second World War, Golden Age fiction fell out of vogue. The cerebral whodunnit was displaced by the psychological thriller. *The Poisoned Chocolates Case* was out of print for decades. It took me years to find a battered second-hand copy.

This struck me as sad. I love modern crime fiction, but that isn't incompatible with loving Golden Age mysteries too. Christie, of course, is an enduring phenomenon, but all my life I've hoped that the merits of her neglected contemporaries would be rediscovered. Thankfully, things have begun to change, and in 2016 I managed to persuade the British Library to reissue Berkeley's masterpiece in their Crime Classics series.

For that edition, I was invited to dream up yet another solution to

Joan's death by chocolate. The opportunity to fashion such a unique personal connection with an author and a novel I've admired for so long was impossible to resist. Luckily, when I read through the story for the umpteenth time, paying close attention to every word, an idea for a fresh murderer and motive sprang to mind. The next challenge was to mimic Berkeley's voice, so that the transition was seamless – or at least as elegant as possible. Writing up the eighth explanation for those poisoned chocs was great fun. Would Berkeley's ghost approve of my coda to his puzzle? Perhaps he might at least be amused.

And now, as we emerge from another global pandemic, is it too much to hope that the escapist, imaginative pleasures of detective fiction past and present will once again help us to cope with life's uncertainties? As we grapple with the mysteries of the real world, a little literary comfort eating won't do us much harm. Nor will devouring a few chocolates. As long as we're sure about where they come from.

MARTIN EDWARDS's lifelong fascination with crime fiction has resulted in twenty novels, most recently *Mortmain Hall* and *The Crooked Shore*, and a library that threatens to take over his home in Cheshire. He has also appeared on our podcast, Episode 33, 'The Golden Age of Crime Writing'.

Return to Sender

MORAG MACINNES

That white ceramic inkpot sitting snugly in the corner of my desk. The agony of a crossed nib. The difficulty, being left-handed, of following the direction 'light on the up stroke, heavy on the down stroke'. The blotting paper. The blue-black permanent stain on my finger. My first pen, an Osmiroid, and a bottle of Quink. I loved lifting the wee lever to refill the pen.

My best friend introduced me to Churlston Deckle. The paper looked as if it was something Moses would have practised his commandments on before he had them engraved. The man I married wrote to me every week – sometimes twice – for four years. That's some correspondence, in a box under the bed.

Now I get a letter once in a blue moon. Emails and texts, yes – but a letter? In a distinctive hand, so you know who sent it before you open it? Those days are gone. It's a shame. Something about the intimacy of the writer's communion with the paper, the space between their thoughts and their pen, the scorings out, the drawings, is precious. A letter in your hand is as intimate as a kiss. It may be marvellous to type thoughts, see them appear like a printed page, but in our heads, as we compose, we are writing in longhand, with our own idiosyncratic script, formed by long dead primary-school teachers. Miss Merriman made me keep a ruler handy in case my writing sloped backwards. If it did, she slapped me on the hand with the same ruler. Hard.

Undelivered Letters to Hudson's Bay Company Men on the Northwest Coast of America, 1830–57 (2003), edited by Helen M. Buss and Judith Hudson Beattie, is out of print but we can obtain second-hand copies.

It's odd, in this interconnected world, to imagine sending a letter to 'the Backside of the World' and having to wait a year for a response. But if your son worked for the Hudson's Bay Company you had no other choice. I've worked for years on a novel about Isobel Gunn, a doughty Orkney woman who dressed as a boy and worked on the Bay 'as hard and well as any of the men' – until she was discovered giving birth on her employer's carpet. It's a remarkable tale, one of many from the beginnings of Empire, when desperate times needed desperate measures.

In the mid-seventeenth century, two Frenchmen, Radisson and des Groseilliers, discovered that North American furs could be sold for vast profit in Europe. Persuaded by his cousin, Prince Rupert, Charles II granted a Royal Charter 'to the Governor and Company of Adventurers of England', giving them a monopoly of trading priv-ileges 'in all those Seas Streights Bayes Lakes Creeks . . . together with all Landes and Territories' accessible via Hudson's Bay. This vague and remarkably presumptuous land grab anointed the Governor and his intrepid trappers 'true and absolute Lordes and Proprietors' of an enormous nation, on payment of two elk and two black beaver should the King happen to visit.

You might think that Arctic fox fur, soft and snowy, was the most popular commodity, but it was the humble beaver who was sacrificed for profit. He had a waterproof coat, perfect for gentlemen's head-gear. Between 80,000 and 100,000 pelts were sent to Britain each year, and in 1690 the Hudson's Bay Company reported, with some complacency, 'our returns in Beaver this year by God's blessing to be worth £20,000'.

Over the next century, wars depleted the manpower available in England. So the man-hungry Company cast its eyes north. Orcadians made ideal Servants, as the Company styled its employees, 'more sober and tractable than the Irish'. They knew how to sail and live off the land. They also lived in dire poverty, so an offer of five years' work for £8 – twice what they could get labouring at home – was tempting. By 1800, nearly 80 per cent of HBC employees were Orcadians. There are, as a result, many Orcadian names in Canadian phone books.

As beaver declined and competition from the French increased, there was a constant need for expansion. Like the East India Company, the HBC became a spider's web of bureaucratic inter-actions controlled by London, sustained by countless reports, instruc-tions – and personal letters. Often, these personal epistles missed their objects. The Servants had finished their service, deserted their ships or died. The Company returned this vagrant post to its London office, and over the years amassed a file of about 250 'undelivered letters' which remained sealed for the next century and a half. Only when the HBC Archives were moved to Canada were the letters opened by the archivist Judith Hudson Beattie, and subsequently published (in 2003) as *Undelivered Letters to Hudson's Bay Company Men on the Northwest Coast of America, 1830–57.*

The contents are fascinating, offering us a unique insight into nineteenth-century life. Real people, spelling in their own dialects, come alive. Clipped ringlets are enclosed. Script crosses and re-crosses the page – post was expensive. Illiterate sweethearts get teachers to write for them. Sisters tease. Mothers are pious, fathers anxious, brothers bawdy.

Take for example the story of the wonderfully named Jonty Buck from Cork. His father Frederick was a miniature portraitist. The Peninsular War had been good to Frederick. He kept a supply of partially painted ivories ready in their gold cases, adding faces and insignia after a brief sitting with departing soldiers. The family was well off but burdened with many children. In 1842 Jonty was Second Mate on a ship bound for the Columbia River. Two years later his mother put together a family package full of news. There's enough in this brief summary to make a novel. Through their letters, the voices of the family flesh out the story.

Matriarch Harriet establishes her character firmly. 'Not a line from

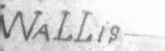

you for twelve long months . . . you are at the time of life to form a character . . . lean on the foundation *Purity Integrity and Sobriety* . . . I hope you are prudent about your money.' She knows him well. She's also aware that she can't control the family narrative. 'I suppose the Boys will each tell their own story . . .' Indeed they do. Adam says, 'I hope there is no fear you will run away with one of those she Indians that you gave such a glowing account of.'

The family is reeling from young Alfred's sudden marriage – 'Just think what an age he has brought the cares of life on him, he is 19 and she 16!' sister Harrietta observes. 'Mama faltered about it but the boys are greatly amused.' Jonty's girlfriend in Innishannon says, 'Was not Alfy's marriage funny? You must not follow his example or I shall be jealous.' Frederick is stiff. 'Mother never told us a word about it until she produced the cake . . . the whole thing is a mystery to me and I don't wish to think of it.' John reports on less personal matters, bad tidings of French revolution – 'the King has abdicated the Throne . . . Guizot the Minister is in the hands of the people and ere now his head off . . .' – and good tidings about the Irish potato famine: 'the winter has passed over without any deaths of starvation'.

We can speculate endlessly about the effect Alfred's behaviour had on the Buck clan, in their close-knit Cork society. Perhaps the last word should go to the miscreant himself. 'A great change has taken place in me,' he tells Jonty. 'I am married . . . she is not 17 years of age yet but very knowing (not at all girlish I mean).' The rest of the letter deals with another man's fraud. Alfred, or Fuzz, as he was known, wanted to divert attention from himself. That nickname signifies he was still barely shaving. Maybe he wanted to be seen as a grown-up.

Jonty never saw his perturbing family news. The invaluable Editors' Notes on the senders and receivers of letters – an enormous exercise in itself – tell us that he deserted at the Sandwich Islands, perhaps in pursuit of a girl, and died in the Gold Rush, digging in California.

The Bucks were a literate, financially stable family. Contrast them with one of the many Orcadian families who feature in this collection, the Hornes, whose descendants still walk the streets of Orkney. Brothers George and Henry set off for Fort Victoria, Vancouver, in 1850. George's sweetheart Isabella fills her letter with local news, and can't resist using her sister to disguise her own insecurity: 'mary sinds kind love to you and tells you not to fall in love with an Indian . . .'

Henry's sweetheart Anne is less literate and less circumspect. She produces a howl of desire, in broad Orcadian. It's a pure stream of consciousness. If I read it aloud I can hear her talking. She brings her lover up to date with local gossip and her travels ('at Glasgo and dundeay ant many more plases'). Now she's back working in the 'lonsome' garret, where clearly she and Henry spent happy private time. 'I wish you was here besid me . . . have you got A swethart where you are I supose you haf got A half a Dousen.' She asks for a lock of his hair, reminding him 'it is wan year an four deas since you left orkney', and ends 'O be sure and writ.'

The Notes tell us she didn't have to worry about Henry's constancy. The brothers came home together, landing in London in 1851, and the following year Anne and Henry married in Orkney.

Not all the stories are as simple. John Spense's letter to an old friend 'on board *Prince Rupert* laying in a five-fathom hole York Factory' hints at the difficulties faced by Servants who married 'in the custom of the Country'. They entered into alliances with First Nation women and had children. This is not surprising, given the lonely nature of the work and the integral part First Nation women played in the smooth functioning of Bay life – netting snowshoes, gutting, canoeing, preparing pelts. The Company had to tolerate it but refused to take financial responsibility for these Country wives. Many were simply abandoned when men had served their time and came back home.

John completed his five years and returned to Orkney; but he had a conscience about the family he'd left behind in Canada: 'Joseph

Give My Compliments to My Old lady . . . I am not married here yet . . . there are plenty girls in Orkney . . . to me they want Money to keep them up, they are remarkably dressy an old fellow like me wanted a Clean Pocket handkerchief every day they dazzled my eyes so.' It's clear he feels out of step, back home. His old First Nation lady would not have had much time for dressing well, and barter would have been her currency.

An open mind about liaisons was the only way for sweethearts waiting at home to cope. Londoner George Barton writes from Canada that he has signed on for another five years, after earning credit for thirty-two hours spent saving a boat locked in ice. His fiancée Maria hopes he won't stay the full term because 'it is a long time to look forward to'. She requests furs, and then says, casually, 'I had allmost forgoten but I suppose your sweetheart and your little Child was very glad to see you again.' Her brother also had a second family on the Bay, according to the Notes; perhaps she was used to the idea. But 'allmost forgoten'? I wonder.

So many stories, saved purely by chance. Reading them makes me realize how close we are to our forebears. I recognize with delight young Edward Wallis who tells his big brother Charles, 'When I come to sea I shall not come as a common sailor but be a captain at once!' He adds a drawing of himself inside a whale. 'This is its ribs,' he has written, helpfully. Then, 'here i am' – a tiny figure, standing firm in the belly. He put pen to paper in Bromley, in September 1847. It could be yesterday.

Maybe it's time to rediscover the hand, the Osmiroid, the intimacy of paper and ink. Get the Churston Deckle out. There's a whole generation who have never had a letter! Anne was wiser than she knew when she told her lover, 'O be sure and writ.'

MORAG MACINNES is an Orcadian writer and lecturer.

A Guest of the Party

DEREK PARKER

After two TV appearances and four radio interviews before 7 a.m., my wife and I were glad we could totter back to the Ambassador in Chicago or the Ritz Carlton in Boston and relax in our suite, lift the telephone and order breakfast for two. But that was half a century ago, when publishers organized publicity tours on a grand scale; now, when friends come to Australia to talk up a new book, I meet them at a hotel (three-star at best) at the back of Kings Cross.

Amor Towles had no accommodation problems during his twenty years as a banker, moving effortlessly from luxury hotel to luxury hotel all across the USA and Europe – and in his spare time writing a novel which was published in 2011 as *Rules of Civility* and immediately entered the bestseller lists. Switching from banking to full-time writing, he continued to frequent grand hotels. One day, sitting in the lobby of one and looking at fellow guests, he had 'this eerie sense that I had seen them before'. He realized that some people actually live, permanently, in hotel suites. 'And I thought, what would it be like to live in a hotel like this for the rest of your life?'

The answer to that question lies at the heart of Towles's second novel, *A Gentleman in Moscow* (2016). For many years Count Alexander Rostov has occupied one of the Moscow Metropol's most luxurious suites. Unmistakably an aristocrat but also a liberal, he supports the 1917 Revolution, but in 1922 he writes a politically equivocal poem which brings him before the Bolshevik Emergency

Amor Towles, *A Gentleman in Moscow* (2016)

Windmill Books · Pb · 512pp · £8.99 · ISBN 9780099558781

Committee of the People's Commissariat for International Affairs. He expects execution, but as he is 'a former hero of the pre-revolutionary cause' the Committee is lenient, and he is sentenced to isolation for the rest of his life within the Metropol. If he sets foot outside the hotel, he will be shot.

Naturally, Rostov cannot continue to occupy the luxurious suite, furnished with handsome family possessions, in which he has previously lived. His furniture is now the property of the people, and he is escorted to a former servants' bedroom under the roof, together with a very few chattels (including, however, a desk the hollow legs of which are stacked with gold coins). There he remains for the duration of the novel, accompanied by Field Marshal Kutuzov, the hotel's one-eyed lobby cat, and occasionally visited by Vasily, the concierge, and Andrey, the maître d' of the famous Boyarsky restaurant. Rostov's lifelong love of food and wine make him especially useful to them when a complaint is filed with the Commissar of Food, claiming that 'the existence of [the hotel's] wine list runs counter to the ideals of the Revolution'. The labels are removed from every one of the 100,000 bottles in the hotel's cellars. Fortunately, Rostov can identify most of them.

The complaint has been made by a new wine waiter, clearly a Party apparatchik, and it seems that the Bolsheviks will not rest until every last vestige of the Metropol Rostov has known and loved has been uprooted, shattered or erased. From that moment, his tolerance of change vanishes, and he decides to rescue the hotel from the revolutionaries.

Unexpected help comes from a 9-year-old girl, Nina Kulikova, living in the hotel with her governess, who presents herself at the Count's luncheon table and eagerly questions him about the lives of former princesses. Incurably curious, she has somehow stolen a hotel passkey, and she introduces him to every corner of the great building. When she leaves, she presents him with the key as a farewell present, and it enables him to enter 'rooms behind rooms and doors behind doors', becoming in all but name the commissar of the Metropol. Using the passkey he familiarizes himself with every aspect of the hotel's changed life, eavesdropping for instance, from the balcony of the magnificent but now dingy ballroom, on the Second Meeting of the First Congress of the Moscow Branch of the All-Russian Union of Railway Workers – that scene is one of several extremely funny contrasts between the increasingly worn elegance of the Metropol and the boorishness of the comrades who are now its chief guests.

This is, incidentally, not only a quietly but also sometimes a quite noisily funny book – when Nina Kulikova first appears accompanied by two elegant borzois, Field Marshal Kutuzov's welcome is less than courteous. Nor is the book devoid of sex: Rostov, clearly an attractive man, is seduced by a young film actress, one moment occupying a magnificent confiscated mansion, the next forced to hand it and its contents back to the people because her latest film has failed to please Stalin. The sound of her silk dress slipping to the floor of the bedroom in the Count's former suite surprises but also delights him.

Rostov has not seen the last of Nina Kulikova: she revisits the hotel as a young woman, her husband sentenced to the Gulag, whence she will follow him. She implores the Count to care for her daughter Sofia. He cannot refuse, and the 5-year-old moves into his tiny apartment. The story of the relationship between the middle-aged aristocrat and the child is both convincing and touching. Sofia turns out to be a spectacularly fine pianist, is fêted in Moscow, longs to play in the West and . . . it is easy to replace the dots. But never mind, the ingenious conclusion will satisfy the most romantic reader.

In any case 'the story' is the least important part of the book. At its core is the relationship between Rostov and the Metropol's staff. No doubt during his early days as a guest he always treated them with courtesy, but now they become his friends, the changing relationship at first rather confusing him, as indeed do the incursions of the outside world: the young second violinist of the trio which plays in the Boyarsky was once the heir of a rich and noble family; the mist of frost on a woman's furs recalls the former world of banquets and balls, seductions and duels (in his time the Count has killed his man).

Outside events and their effects are not central to the story, only rarely seriously disturbing, and never dominating its flow, yet the changes in society are continually reflected in the presence and behaviour of the *nouveau puissant* guests, who can't read the menu, order red wine with fish and gesture rudely with their forks. Apropos, one day a mysterious stranger summons the Count to dinner. He is a Colonel in the Red Army, 'an officer of the Party', whose task, he says, is to 'keep track of certain men of interest'. In fact he has come to commission Rostov to teach him how to be 'a gentleman'. Clearly, things are changing.

And indeed, in 1953, Stalin dies. Gradually, the country opens up: foreign correspondents appear at the hotel, a few high-ranking American officers, even one or two tourists. From the Metropol's windows the Count sees across Theatre Square that the audience arriving at the Bolshoi is once again in evening dress. In the Metropol's kitchen, the chef can once more complete his recipes using real ingredients rather than rough equivalents picked from neglected gardens. And the man they call The Butler, clearly a Party spy, loses most of his unspoken authority.

You can stay at the Metropol today: an excellent suite will cost you about 33,500 roubles (say £350) a night. I have been unable to obtain an estimate for a single room under the eaves. Dining in the main restaurant under its stained-glass dome I doubt if you will need a black tie; nor would I expect to find many diners clad in the 'simple, hygienic and functional clothes' of the Revolutionary period. But I would not be surprised should a tall, elegant man of impeccable carriage, greying perhaps a little at the temples, be promptly at your side to advise, discreetly, that 'a bottle of the San Lorenzo Barolo 1912 Mukuzani will be excellent with the osso buco'.

DEREK PARKER has just returned from an 18-year holiday in Australia, and is testing King George V's opinion of life in Bognor.

In Pursuit of an Ideal

SUE GEE

On 1 January 1913 a new kind of bookshop opened in London. Located in a rundown street off Theobalds Road, it occupied three floors of a Georgian house, and was presided over by an idealist whose private income – largely derived from family-owned asylums – never quite met the shop's expenses. This was Harold Monro, poet, publisher and editor of *The Poetry Review*, to whose subscribers he announced his intention of opening a bookshop 'devoted to the sale of poetry, and of all books, pamphlets and periodicals connected with poetry'. For the next two decades he was to put the Poetry Bookshop at the heart of the London poetry scene. The other figure bestriding literary London at this time was Ezra Pound: in temperament, taste and ambition the two men could not have been more different.

Devonshire Street (now Boswell Street) was dark and narrow, once described by Osbert Sitwell as 'given over to screaming children, lusty small boys armed with catapults, and to leaping flights of eighteenth-century cats'. Alida Monro, Harold's second wife and most assuredly his saviour, described 'a slum street . . . the passerby in constant peril of being hit on the head by kipper bones and banana skins falling from upper windows'. There were three pubs, and the policemen patrolled in pairs.

Elegant though its proportions were, it was brave indeed for Harold Monro to take the lease of No. 35 and hang over the front

---

Joy Grant, *Harold Monro and the Poetry Bookshop* (1967), is out of print but we can obtain second-hand copies.

door a swinging sign in bold black letters announcing THE POETRY BOOKSHOP. But he knew what he was doing.

'The piquant idea of a poetry shop in a slum street took people's fancy,' writes Joy Grant, author of *Harold Monro and the Poetry Bookshop* (1967). I was led to this book by my interest in the poet Charlotte Mew, befriended to the end of her tragic life by Alida and Harold. Grant writes wonderfully well about the couple's marriage, the bookshop and its times, and is an astute critic of Monro's own poetry and of the many poets he published and encouraged. She is also pleasingly dry – 'Miss Webster wrote soft female poetry of the heart' – and often made me laugh. The book has a few fine photographs and is altogether a delight.

Who was Harold Monro? Tall, dark, and described by Grant as 'very faintly saturnine', he was born in Brussels in 1879, the son of a civil engineer, and came to England when he was 6. At 16 he was expelled from Radley for sneaking a bottle of something into his study. 'By a stroke of good fortune I left school young,' is how he put it in an unpublished memoir. He retreated to his bedroom, writing poems and stories 'all about an individual too obviously myself . . . By the time I went to Cambridge poetry had become an obsession.' There, he read everything from Virgil to Keats, via Goethe, Molière and Milton, and began to take his own poetry seriously.

By the time he founded the Poetry Bookshop at the age of 34, he had dropped out of law school, travelled extensively in Europe, come under the influence of Edward Carpenter, Walt Whitman's English heir, married his best friend's sister, had a son, taken them to Ireland and returned, finding it very wet. It seems this first marriage foundered on his need simply to go his own way. Monro was a complex individual. A romantic idealist inspired by Shelley, he was part of that early to mid-twentieth century strand of thinking, secular and utopian, which looked back to Tolstoy, Ruskin and William Morris, and forward to a society rid of industrial capitalism. He searched all his life for the poetic language in which to express himself, often failing.

His love of dogs, the seasons, the earth, the English countryside and domestic life put him in the camp of what Grant describes as 'the pleasant inanities' of much Georgian poetry, yet he was also aware that by the turn of the century he and those like him were 'at the end of an outworn tradition'. 'Oh, this fearful minor key!' he wrote once. 'This is an age of clipped wings and misty intelligences!'

He struggled with Modernism, and as a publisher turned down both Edward Thomas and T. S. Eliot. In turn, Ezra Pound rejected one of Monro's own poems for an Imagist collection because 'he clung to an adjective'. 'His tragedy', writes Grant, 'was not that he liked what was bad, but that he failed to respond sufficiently to what was good.'

There were other tragedies. He suffered from ill health, and he drank too much, perhaps to drown a fundamental loneliness: since Radley, he had known that he was homosexual. He had a serious, lifelong struggle with the idea of God. It was the Poetry Bookshop, and his marriage to the much younger woman who came to work there, that gave him purpose and fulfilment.

Alida Klemantski became Monro's secretary late in 1913. Of Polish descent, gifted, beautiful and well-read, she had intended to become a doctor, and rescue prostitutes. Instead, she rescued him, bringing her own sensitive literary judgement to publications, and a calm efficiency to book-keeping and the dispatch of orders. 'Miss Klemantski is just splendid, and understands everything,' he told a friend. It was she who kept the shop running all through the war, while he was working in the Intelligence Department of the War Office. They were married in 1920, by then well established as an appealing and immensely hospitable couple.

With its custom-made oak bookshelves and settles, literary reviews spread on the tables, a coal fire in winter and Harold's beloved cat before it, the bookshop was a perfect place for browsing and conversation. A huge amount went on there, Harold directing operations from his office on the first floor. Between 1911 and 1922 he published seven volumes of Georgian poetry (it was he who coined the term) edited by Edward Marsh, which at their best brought Robert Bridges, Edward Thomas, Walter de la Mare, Siegfried Sassoon and D. H. Lawrence to a newly eager readership. For a long time, it was the sale of these volumes that kept the bookshop afloat.

There were also individual collections, often by women, including Frances Cornford, Eleanor Farjeon and Charlotte Mew, as well as chapbooks – economically priced miniature paper-bound volumes with strong, simple cover designs. These were intended, wrote Monro, 'to be sold anywhere and everywhere, carried in the pocket, read at any spare moment, left in the train'. This is how Robert Graves's first collection was published. Monro also published delightful rhyme sheets – individual poems (from Dryden to de la Mare) typeset on long thin strips of paper and decorated by artists: Paul Nash, James Guthrie, David Jones. The novelist Penelope Fitzgerald cherished the ones she had as a child, pinning them up on her bedroom wall.

And then there were the readings. These were held in an old outhouse; occasionally rain blew in. They were not advertised: you picked up who was reading next week from chat in the shop. 'Anyone who wishes to stroll in may do so,' Monro had airily announced, though he admitted that this sometimes meant 'the most extraordinary people'. Once inside, paying threepence to sixpence, the audience was seated in rows before a green-shaded lamp on a reading desk. Monro stepped out from behind a curtain with what one man recalled as 'a stiff little soldierly bow, and the suspicion of a smile', and introduced the evening's poets.

Both he and Alida were tremendous readers; Monro believed that poetry could be properly understood only by being read aloud, and he gathered here everyone from Yeats and Edith Sitwell to Joyce, Pound and Eliot, via many a keen but lesser voice. Rupert Brooke read several

times to a packed house, once before the war, looking like 'an annun-
ciating angel', and once in July 1914, with a streaming cold. 'Speak up,
young man,' came a stern female voice. By the autumn he was in
uniform, drawn and disheartened, talking only of the war.

Not everyone wanted to read their own work, and Alida was
happy to step in for the shy and hesitant. One such was Charlotte
Mew. Alida found her, Harold published her, and in so doing showed
his judgement at its best, for Mew was writing anything but 'soft
female poetry of the heart'. His yardstick was 'Did this poem have to
be written?' Could there be a better? Wilfred Owen wrote to his
mother in 1916 of Monro's skilful editing of his work. 'He went over
the things in detail and he told me what was fresh and clever, and
what was second-hand and banal, and what Keatsian and what
"modern" . . . I need not say that he is a peculiar being . . .'

In truth, through this enriching book, I rather fell for Monro. In
1926, with failing health and eyesight, and the lease on Devonshire
Street at an end, he moved the bookshop to Great Russell Street, a
much better location but without the same atmosphere. No matter.
By the time of his death in 1932 he had created a marvellously wel-
coming and convivial place, published some of the most important
poets in the English language, and worked tirelessly in pursuit of an
ideal: poetry at the very heart of life. Through it all he was, writes
Grant, 'an unhappy human being groping nervously towards the
expression of his inner life'.

Though Joy Grant's inclusion and analysis of Monro's poetry is
much too long, he did leave some work of considerable merit. Philip
Larkin recognized this, including in *The Oxford Book of Twentieth
Century English Verse* (1973) 'Thistledown', much more subtle than it
seems on first reading, and 'Midnight Lamentation', a poem to break
your heart.

SUE GEE's collection of essays, *Just You and the Page: Encounters with Twelve
Writers*, is published by Seren Books. She can also be heard discussing the art of
editing on our podcast, Episode 3, 'Stet'.

Between Limerick and London

ANDY BOURNE

'Any man who would see another man's glass empty is a bastard.' This is the first commandment of Stanley Callaghan, one of many wonderful characters created by Michael Curtin, a comic genius sadly recognized as such only by a discerning few, though his fellow Irishman Roddy Doyle described him as 'one of Ireland's very best writers', and they do say that it takes one to know one.

I was first introduced to Curtin's brilliantly realized and eccentric world almost forty years ago. My then flatmate Harry, an unusual character himself who would not have been entirely out of place in Curtin's work, had come across his novel *The Replay* (1981). Usually the most loquacious of men, Harry was rendered speechless for the best part of twenty-four hours while reading it – apart from splutterings of manic laughter and occasional shouts of 'You have to read this when I'm finished.' I did so, and was up all night. I was devastated when I finished it, but then overjoyed to discover that it was Curtin's second novel. I duly found, and devoured, his first, *The Self-Made Men* (1980). Then I had to wait a few years for Curtin to write another one, but thankfully he did. In fact he wrote another four.

Michael Curtin died in 2016, so sadly it seems there will be no more (I say 'seems' because when he died he left behind the uncompleted manuscript of his seventh novel, so I live in hope that one day,

---

Michael Curtin's *The Self-Made Men* (1980), *The Replay* (1981), *The League against Christmas* (1989), *The Plastic Tomato Cutter* (1991), *The Cove Shivering Club* (1996), and *Sing!* (2001) are all out of print, but we can try to obtain second-hand copies.

somehow, it will be published), but the six novels we do have are up there with the very best of Irish comic writing. The *Sunday Express*, reviewing his fifth book, *The Cove Shivering Club* (1996), described him perfectly. 'Curtin is one of Ireland's national treasures, a superb comic writer who deserves to be better known.'

Those who do know him read him not just for the gorgeous craziness of his storytelling but also for his powers of description. Whether his characters are in Limerick or London, you are right there with them, in the pub, in the park or on the street. Curtin himself once said that in the event of a nuclear bomb falling on his beloved Limerick, it should be possible to rebuild the city from his books, in the same way that Joyce's Dublin could be reconstructed by following Leopold Bloom's meanderings in *Ulysses*. So, for the uninitiated, allow me to be your guide on what will be a very brief tour. We will take it in historical order – a very 'un-Curtin-like' approach, for tinkering with the chronology is one of this writer's favourite comic tricks.

We will start, as he did, with *The Self-Made Men*, which begins thus: 'Ten years earlier Billy Whelan had twelve hundred pounds on deposit with Barclays and yet managed to starve on Christmas Day.' It is soon obvious that the book is as mad as its hero, Billy Whelan. But, once Curtin has lured you into his web, Billy seems like the sanest man you have ever met. When he asks Breda, the most beautiful woman in the world, to marry him after knowing her for less than ten minutes, you are by this stage so deep into his reality that not only does his proposal seem perfectly sensible, you even feel it would be foolish of her to refuse. I won't reveal whether or not she marries him, but please don't go thinking this is a straightforward romantic narrative. Things get seriously strange, in the most hilarious way.

I've already mentioned the great Stanley Callaghan, hero of Curtin's second novel, *The Replay*. Stanley is the captain, and charismatic leader, of the strangest crew of pub footballers you could

possibly imagine. And no, you don't have to like or understand football to love this book, but you will grow to love Stanley Callaghan,
an old-fashioned man madly in love with his wife Kate, who, because
of his strict sense of honour, accepts a challenge to replay a match
from fifteen years ago – a match which his eccentric bunch of misfits,
has-beens and ne'er-do-wells clearly cannot win. Not least because
one of them now weighs over twenty stone, another has been com-
mitted to a psychiatric hospital, a third has an arm in plaster having
been kicked down the stairs by his wife, and a fourth is suffering
from the considerable disadvantage of being dead. And no substi-
tutes are allowed. So no, of course they can't win. Can they?

I worried at times, during my seven years of waiting for his next
book, whether Curtin could possibly follow *The Replay*. But follow it
he did, magnificently, with *The League against Christmas* (1989). Here
the plot is not so much convoluted as corkscrewed, and features a
cast (or perhaps a gang) including an ex-bank manager with a fetish
for linoleum, a cross-dressing accountant, a barman with a morbid
fear of winning the football pools, and the impossibly glamorous
owner of a glossy women's magazine, all of whom are under surveil-
lance by an increasingly paranoid police force convinced they are
dealing with a fiendishly clever terrorist plot. In reality, the group's
purpose is much stranger than even the police can imagine. A quote
may help to give the flavour, without giving the game away: "'You
don't care for Christmas, Ellis?' "Foster, if Christmas was a person I
would go out on a foggy night and cut its throat and then I'd hand
myself in and happily spend the rest of my life watching videos in
prison . . .'"

Next came what some aficionados consider to be Curtin's best –
The Plastic Tomato Cutter (1991) – which contains not one but two of
his finest comic creations. The marvellous Mr Yendall, perhaps the
ultimate purveyor of the 'Modern life is rubbish' theory, watches
with horror as social change begins to engulf his traditional world.
Meanwhile Tim Harding is running an organization called Fagenders,

ostensibly helping smokers to quit, while nipping out the back for a crafty fag between sessions. And, in keeping with Curtin's love of esoteric pastimes, Harding does a spot of bell-ringing on the side, which he takes very seriously, as bell-ringers do. Not many novels feature bell-ringing – offhand, apart from *The Hunchback of Notre-Dame*, I can only think of Dorothy L. Sayers's *The Nine Tailors*, also an excellent book, even if Sayers's bell-ringers, though all potentially murderous, lack the terrifyingly deadpan insanity of Curtin's.

For bell-ringing, read swimming in *The Cove Shivering Club* (1996), Curtin's penultimate novel. The first paragraph, voiced by the book's protagonist, writer Junior Nash, reels you in seductively, while (as is often the case in Curtin-land) hinting at the life of the author himself:

> The dust jackets of my books proclaim the usual codswallop: clerk, bus conductor, factory hand, builder's labourer, barman, burden on the state. Yet if the midnight knock ever comes to my door and I blink awake into the truncheons and the barrels of the guns and hear the bark: What are you?, Junior Nash is likely to come back with: I'm a swimmer.

Of course Junior Nash is much more than just a swimmer, or just a writer, and Curtin breathes life into him and his fellow Shivering Club members with loving care.

Curtin's last novel, *Sing!* (2001), is the most bittersweet of his books, at times much more bitter than sweet. Jimmy Imbusch, better known as Toots Books, the name of the shop where he very occasionally gets round to selling a book, is desperate to get his wife Nellie to return to him from the convent to which she has exiled herself following a family tragedy. But how to accomplish this? Toots and his friends decide to stage an old-fashioned variety concert to tempt Nellie back through the medium of her love of music. There is though (as you may have guessed) a small problem. All Toots's friends – Jack Droney, who likes to recite dramatic monologues to fields of cows, Ignatius Valelly, 'who never once dirtied his brains for a living', Madeleine Brown, alcoholic ex-queen of the university debating society, and Walter Nix, failed police informant and detective fiction addict – are as mad as a box of frogs, and about as reliable. And Toots's own sanity is on the fragile side. So can they pull off the concert? And if they can, will Nellie come home to Toots? Well, that would be telling.

You will have gathered by now that I am a huge fan of Curtin's work, but I would not pretend he is perfect. At times he gets carried away and overwrites – 'loses the run of himself' as they say in Ireland – and it could be argued that a firmer editorial hand might have made one or two of these fine books even better. But I am delighted this did not happen. It would have been a sad loss if his tremendous flights of fancy had been curtailed by caution, and I would far rather have too much of his exuberance than too little.

I should also acknowledge that my love for Michael Curtin may well have a personal element. A Venn diagram representing some of his archetypes (people caught between Irish and English cultures, people with a tendency to drink too much, smoke too much and spend too much time in pubs with sticky carpets, people who have old-school attitudes as to how life might best be enjoyed and endured, and hold, shall we say, unpredictable attitudes to authority) would have me placed at several intersections. But I'm fine with that. Above all, I stand with Stanley Callaghan when he says, 'Any man who would see another man's glass empty is a bastard.' So please, raise your glasses and join me in a toast to Michael Curtin, and to his brave, battered, baffled crew, as they struggle to make sense of this bizarre but beguiling world.

ANDY BOURNE now lives in Devon, after many years in Galway on the west coast of Ireland. He writes fiction and non-fiction, with the encouragement of his partner and their cat.

Hell and Good Intentions

SUE GILD

It was the title that first attracted me, so many years ago. What adventure-hungry 13-year-old girl could resist *On Sledge and Horseback to Outcast Siberian Lepers*? My first love, Huck Finn, was overthrown within minutes. He was just a boy who had floated down a river on a raft; this was a young woman, a heroine, who had braved wolves, bandits and terrible hardships in a noble cause. And it was a true story! I longed to be Kate Marsden and ride through the Siberian wastes, a handsome Russian officer at my side. It was not to be: the book, borrowed from an elderly aunt, vanished during a house move and eventually real life supplanted schoolgirl dreams.

Then, two years ago, while rummaging in a second-hand book-shop, my eye was caught by a book whose cover showed a team of horses racing wildly through a snowstorm, a light timber sledge bucking behind them and wolves at their heels. Here was my lost book, reprinted and with the added bonus of a preface by that other intrepid traveller, Eric Newby. Immediately I was under the spell of that remarkable woman again.

Kate Marsden was born in 1859. Little is known of her early life except that, aged 19, she served as a nurse in the Russo-Turkish War. There she first came across lepers and was told, to her horror, that they were shunned and despised in many places: 'There is no cure – the best remedy is to shoot them – poison them – anything to put them out of their misery.' She vowed to devote her life to caring for

---

Kate Marsden, *On Sledge and Horseback to Outcast Siberian Lepers* (1893), is out of print but we can obtain second-hand copies.

lepers and when, a decade later, she heard of a herb said to alleviate the symptoms of leprosy, she determined to travel to the only place it could be found – Yakutsk, in the depths of Siberia.

The account of her extraordinary expedition opens in Moscow in 1890, where Kate and a female friend (whom she has somehow persuaded to accompany her) arrive in icy mid-winter. She hopes to raise interest and funds for the 5,000-mile trek to Yakutsk, but she faces setbacks from the beginning: despite letters of introduction from the Queen and the Princess of Wales, she is suspected of being a spy. Eventually, however, she succeeds in attracting the patronage of members of the Russian aristocracy and starts to plan the journey. Endearingly, she admits that this provides a moment of excitement and pleasure (she is, after all, only 31 and has a lively interest in clothes): 'Even my own attention, I must confess, was diverted from the lepers for a moment in thinking what to wear,' and the list of capes, furs and woollen undergarments is a long one. As to provisions, they included 40 lbs of plum pudding, 'because I like it, and it keeps well'.

At last, armed with a letter from the Empress, she is ready to set off: but it quickly becomes obvious that, wrapped as she is in layer upon layer of heavy clothes, she cannot climb up into the sledge. Before a humiliatingly large crowd of onlookers she has to be hoisted into it by some muscular policemen, then 'packed and stowed away' before the driver will take his seat. Luckily Kate is blessed with a sense of humour and a sense of the ridiculous, and this is a moment of light relief before the appalling discomfort to come.

The post-houses where she and her companion stop at night are bare and stinking, the walls crawling with bugs, but welcome even so after a day in the horse-drawn sledge: 'You ache from head to foot; you are bruised all over; your poor brain throbs until you give way to a kind of hysterical outcry . . .' The driver yells constantly and whips the horses on, 'but, oh, for five minutes' peace! Bumping, jolting, tossing; heaved, pitched and thumped.'

Things improve markedly when a Russian soldier called Popoff is appointed to assist her: 'When we came to post-houses it was often a problem with me, weighted and hampered as I was with so many clothes and wraps, how to scramble out of the sledge without assistance: but this man stretched out his hands, and I just tumbled into them, furs and all.' He helps her off with her furs and high boots and serves her devotedly, and she declares that she would trust him with her life. He is, however, 'only a common soldier', and at Omsk the Governor decides that she needs a more suitable escort. He appoints Petroff, a military attaché, to join the expedition.

Petroff speaks French and a little English and proves invaluable, for Kate speaks no Russian and her companion, who has acted as interpreter, has become so ill she has had to leave the expedition. Petroff accompanies Kate for the entire way and attests to her account of the journey in the Appendix. (Despite my romantic imaginings when I first read this in my early teens, there seems to be no hint of any indiscretion – and indeed how could there have been, sewn as she was into her woollen and fur-lined armour of chastity?)

On and on plunges the expedition, over icy tracks and swollen rivers. When at last she arrives, exhausted, in Yakutsk, she describes it with wry understatement as 'not a pretty place'. Yakutsk is one of the coldest places in the world, where in winter the temperature drops to minus 58°C. 'Even one's eyelashes freeze,' she notes, 'so that it is almost impossible to see.' Here there is a moment of delight at last when she is given a specimen of the miraculous herb. Encouraged, she determines to travel to Viluisk (now Vilyuysk), hundreds of miles north-west of Yakutsk, where there are reports of lepers living in terrible conditions, and only one doctor to care for 70,000 people in an area larger than France. She will do what she can to alleviate the immediate suffering of the unfortunate lepers and report on the practicality of establishing a hospital.

By the time she is re-provisioned and ready to set out it is early summer. The ice has melted, temperatures are soaring and the swamps and marshes swarm with mosquitoes and flies. One reads on in fascinated horror. There are bears, wolves, a forest fire . . . and everywhere she finds gangs of convicts held in appalling conditions and pitiful lepers, abandoned, starving, with no medical care or, indeed, any other human contact. As she hands out packets of tea and bibles, even Kate's fortitude is tried. 'Some of the worst details are too repulsive to write about, even for the sake of increasing sympathy for the lepers,' she notes. Her health of course breaks down and when, nearly a year after the start of her journey, she arrives back in Moscow she is exhausted.

On her return to England Kate wrote the account of her journey in order to raise awareness of the state of the lepers and to raise money for their relief. *On Sledge and Horseback*, published in 1893, was not met with great acclaim: many frankly did not believe that a single young woman could have endured such hardships. Had she made it all up? Popular fiction at the time was full of stories of women battling through forests, escaping savages, enduring starvation; and in her novel *I Would Be Private*, Rose Macaulay, herself a serious traveller, poked fun at the genre.

Surprisingly, Eric Newby too fails to do Kate justice. He dismisses her in his preface as a middle-aged nurse and missionary enamoured of the rich and royal, and suggests there is no evidence that her journey achieved anything. Newby made light of his own hair-raising experiences in India and Afghanistan, and I suspect he found her rather earnest.

What in the end happened to Kate? Were we to believe that she retired to leafy suburban Surrey and joined a knitting circle, conscientiously sending Christmas parcels of hand-knitted socks to long-abandoned leper colonies? As a teenager I preferred to imagine that she returned to a true heroine's welcome and married the dashing and adoring Russian officer who had accompanied her through so many near-disasters. In fact the truth is even more satisfying: she raised a great deal of money which enabled her to found the St Francis Leprosy Guild – a charity which still exists – and she continued to work for many years to alleviate the plight of lepers. She was also elected as a Fellow of the Royal Geographical Society.

Sadly, Kate's story does not end well. There was continuing controversy over her account of her journey, allegations of misuse of funds and suggestions of homosexuality. In desperation she wrote *My Mission in Siberia: A Vindication* (1921), and subsequent investigations cleared her of any wrongdoing, but her reputation was tarnished. She never recovered her health and died, an invalid, in 1931.

The essence of a good adventure story is that it fires the imagination. Kate Marsden's book did just that and planted in me a lifelong fascination with other courageous and independent women travellers – Mary Kingsley, Isabella Bird, Freya Stark, to name just a few – but these women were, in general, motivated by a lively curiosity and the excitement of exploration and discovery. There can be no doubt that Kate Marsden's motives were purely altruistic, inspired by her compassion for the abandoned and suffering untouchables. It is this warmth and generosity of spirit that shines through her story and makes the book so unforgettable.

Having abandoned her dream of tracking the Siberian wastes, SUE GILD became in turn journalist, caterer and law lecturer before retiring to the warmth of southwest France.

Bowled Over by Bunkle

ANDREW BOWDEN

Bunkle began it for me. Searching for a gentle, undemanding get-me-to-sleep read, I happened on my wife's childhood copy of a book called *Bunkle Began It* by Margot Pardoe. On a quick skim, I discovered that it was set in a seaside town on the edge of Exmoor which was my own home territory during the war. It also took me back to a *Children's Hour* play with Bunkle as the lead character which had scared the wits out of me but was compulsive listening.

However, this book wasn't exactly soporific; in fact I was still deep in it at 2 a.m. It was fun, it was realistic, it was well-written and it was a real page-turner. Its hero is a gloriously anarchic schoolboy, 10 years old when we first meet him, who is unsquashable, unafraid, his own person, a fluent linguist, with a talent for getting himself into and out of trouble. He is attractively unpretentious and has a natural talent for getting on with people. His real name is Billy, but his older siblings call him Bunkle 'because he talks such bunk'. I can think of only two people I've ever met who were remotely like him, but Bunkle is a wholly endearing and believable character.

He is also part of an equally believable family. It is 1940 and his father, Major de Salis, is a wartime James Bond in what would now

---

Margot Pardoe, *Four Plus Bunkle* (1939), *Bunkle Began It* (1942), *Bunkle's Brainwave* (1952), *Bunkle Scents a Clue* (1953) and *Bunkle Brings It Off* (1961) are available in paperback from Fidra Books. *Bunkle Butts In* (1943), *Bunkle Bought It* (1945), *Bunkle Breaks Away* (1947), *Bunkle and Belinda* (1948), *Bunkle Baffles Them* (1949), *Bunkle Went for Six* (1950) and *Bunkle Gets Busy* (1951) are out of print.

be called MI6, a quick-reacting operator who thinks outside the box and is sent all over the country to investigate what is going on 'when funny things start to happen'. He is also a parent who listens to his children, trusts them and expects them to act as sensible adults. Mrs de Salis has to balance following the maverick movements of her husband with looking after three teenagers. She is somewhat given to retiring to bed with a headache, but she trusts her children and believes that they need challenge and adventure.

Jill, the oldest, is 17, and often left in charge. An uncertain teenager, still at the stage of blushing to the roots of her hair when having to 'entertain' a handsome young Royal Tank Regiment officer, she is weighed down by the burden of responsibility for her brothers. Robin is 14 and leads the 'Bunkle needs to be squashed' campaign: but he is still very ready to horse about with his younger brother, and when it comes to 'adventuring' they do things together.

So, unlike the Browns in *Just William*, this is a family team. These are not books about 'the children' but about young people against the background of their family and their society.

Bunkle Began It was published in 1942, and exactly captures the topsy-turvy unsettledness of those early war years. The food is awful, every second person is in uniform, service families are forever on the move, and *there are spies everywhere!* The de Salises are holed up in a small family hotel in Minehead, and the claustrophobic awfulness of such institutions in those days, alleviated only by the simple kindness of the local staff, is graphically described. Bunkle has discovered a passage to the cisterns under the attic eaves and he and Robin go exploring.

'Hello,' said Bunkle, 'There's quite a big hole here. It goes down beside one of the pipes. You can see down right into the bedroom below. I wonder whose room it is?'

'Here, let me have a look,' said Robin.

'You can only see down if you lie absolutely flat and get your eye right against the pipe. It's just like looking through a hole in a curtain.'

'No, you can't see a lot,' agreed Robin. 'I can see the corner of a table, and what looks like a drawing spread out on it. It must be the edge of the dressing table I think, because I can see the strut of a mirror, and there's something most peculiar hanging on it.'

'My turn,' said Bunkle firmly. 'Move over. Yes I can see it too now. What on earth can it be?' Then he began to giggle. 'Oh glory. I know. It's a wig!'

The ancient residents resent the appearance in their midst of these exuberant teenagers – and the feeling is mutual. The residents are joined by a character who is even older, more bad-tempered and more unhinged. Mrs Wetherby has red hair and a pug dog, she carries around a suspicious roll of tapestry and *she wears gloves which she never takes off.* When she catches Bunkle hiding under the table in her room he discovers that she has a startlingly strong grip and terrifying eyes. Even the fearless Bunkle is frightened.

There have been 'funny things going on in the area' – flashing lights from a deserted house up on the hill, an unidentified German plane that streaks down the Bristol Channel hotly pursued by Spitfires – and there is an information leak. Major de Salis, who arrives for a week's leave, is determined to do 'a little quiet snooping'. Hearing that the local Home Guard is planning a live ammunition exercise in the area, he takes the family on a hike over Exmoor to investigate.

They are challenged by a suspiciously officious member of the Home Guard; and later, under cover of firing during the 'Exercise', someone takes a pot-shot at the Major. Meanwhile, by an ingenious use of mirrors, Bunkle and Robin uncover Mrs Wetherby's secret.

It may sound a bit like an Enid Blyton *Famous Five* adventure, but it is in a different league. *Bunkle Began It* is the second book in the Bunkle series and when I'd finished it I was desperate for more, but

they were hard to find. After a lengthy search I discovered that Fidra Books has reprinted five of them with the original illustrations by Julie Neild, Mary Smith and others, though the rest are, sadly, out of print.

Why are they so good? For a start the characters are human and believable, and as the series develops they grow up. Bunkle starts out as a bumptious 10-year-old in *Four Plus Bunkle* (1939) and ends in *Bunkle Scents a Clue* (1953) as a 17-year-old showing distinct signs of maturity. I particularly liked his first boy-girl encounter in *Bunkle Breaks Away* (1947). Bunkle is doing a holiday job as a waiter in a riverside pub where he works alongside the waitress Carrie, who rather falls for him. She is persuaded to come with him to the nearby woods at dusk, only to find that all he wants to do is to show her the marvellous evening gathering of thousands of starlings.

Part of the books' attraction lies in their accurate picture of unpretentious middle-class life and the political background of the 1940s and 1950s: the period of the Second World War and the Cold War are the instantly recognizable context for the 'adventures'. And their settings are well researched and skilfully evoked. Even today you can trace the *Bunkle Began It* Exmoor scenes – the bus journeys and hikes – on a 2½-inch Ordnance Survey map. And I could take you to the Quantock coombs and the disused iron-mining railway behind Watchet, which are the vividly described settings for *Bunkle Scents a Clue*. Other books are set in France, Scotland and Hampshire, and it is evident that the author has been there herself. In fact the second half of *Bunkle Gets Busy* (1951) is not a bad travel guide to the area of France around Lourdes.

Then there's the style – not over-adult but not dumbed down either. Here's a passage from *Bunkle Scents a Clue* which well illustrates Margot Pardoe's delight in a countryside she knows and loves.

Nearer at hand the ground fell away in a series of curves towards the wide strip of fertile farmland lying between the ridge of the Brendons and the sea. The slopes and fields and wooded valleys seemed to be spread out like a coloured carpet, for every shade of green was there, with vivid splashes of plough-land brick red in the sun, while to the east the smiling range of the Quantock hills, looking misty blue along their crests, ran southwards toward Taunton.

Once you've started a Bunkle book you won't want to put it down. It's not that there is a cliff-hanger on every page, but Pardoe knows how to tell a good story. In the early book *Bunkle Began It*, she uses the obvious trick of ending each chapter with a surprise; but later in the series, in *Bunkle Scents a Clue* for instance, the design is more sophisticated. The human story lures us in, but always, dropped in quietly and persistently, are questions we want answered, and mysteries that need to be explained.

Margot Pardoe produced a new book every year, and would sometimes write one in a fortnight. She rarely revised a manuscript, which does mean that the books can be uneven, and indeed some of the plots peter out. Pat, who is nearly kidnapped because her scientist father is escaping from a laboratory in one of the Iron Curtain countries, is the catalyst for the whole 'adventure' in *Bunkle Gets Busy*. But after the climax, when the Communist agent with his pistol has been floored by a splendid rugby tackle by Robin, we never actually discover what happens to Pat and her family in the future. But it's still a 'ripping good yarn'.

Vanessa Robertson's introduction to the Fidra editions tells us that Margot Pardoe was born in London in 1902, that she studied music in Paris but then turned to writing poetry and articles for journals. She married John Swift, a schoolmaster, in 1934 and they had one son. They soon moved to Selworthy on the edge of Exmoor to set up a country-house hotel. Her first children's novel, *The Far Island*, was published in 1936, with a good review in the *Times Literary Supplement*, and this was followed in 1939 by the first of the Bunkle books. The couple kept the hotel going during the difficult war years, but in the 1950s John became ill, and for a time they lived in Switzerland (the setting for *Bunkle Gets Busy*).

During the 1940s the Bunkle books became very popular, and four were serialized on *Children's Hour*. Not surprisingly they went out of fashion in the 1960s, and *Bunkle Brings It Off*, published in 1961, was Margot Pardoe's last book. But perhaps we are now far enough away from that time for a new generation to enjoy them.

ANDREW BOWDEN is a retired rural parish priest living in Gloucestershire. He loves rediscovering children's books and is an avid collector. He has also written a few books about the rural church, which have been well received but are never likely to feature in *Slightly Foxed*.

Not While It's Running

POSY FALLOWFIELD

My father used to tell a story about a Frenchman (the dependable butt of Edwardian jokes) being invited to some large estate for a shoot. Seeing a cock pheasant coming into the open and running alongside a wood, he levels his gun to aim at it. At which his English host says, 'My dear man, you can't shoot it while it's running!' The Frenchman replies, 'Certainly not, I shall wait until it stops.' This used to make my father fall about laughing but I could never understand why.

Matters of Edwardian etiquette are central to Isabel Colegate's novel *The Shooting Party* (1980). It is set in 1913, a year of agonizing significance, on an 8,000-acre country estate owned by Sir Randolph Nettleby, and the action takes place in the course of a day, the third of a three-day shoot. Various elegant and affluent guests constitute the house party; Minnie, Sir Randolph's wife, supervises the catering and the entertainment down to the last detail; the household staff ensure everything runs like clockwork; the gamekeeper has planned and brought off a superb three days' sport – but due to a breach of etiquette the day ends with an obscenely shocking, unforeseen, tragedy.

Etiquette – or the 'customs of the tribe', as Colegate refers to it at one point – crops up repeatedly; one of the guests is upset at having the wrong shirt studs with him, and when his wife accuses him of being ridiculous, he replies: 'It's all very well. Dismiss these things if you like, but they are the structure of our lives and if we lose respect for them we lose respect for ourselves.'

Isabel Colegate, *The Shooting Party* (1980)
Penguin · Pb · 224pp · £9.99 · ISBN 9780141188676

Etiquette dictates, for the hostess Minnie, that certain guests known to be conducting an extra-marital affair are invited together; etiquette dictates that sport is not a subject for conversation when ladies are present; etiquette dictates that shooting must never be competitive. It also dictates what you can and cannot shoot: while rabbits are described as 'thoroughly sporting little beasts', on no account can you shoot deer. When a terrified roe deer bursts out of the undergrowth in front of the line of guns, Tibor Rakassyi, a Hungarian count not completely at ease among his English hosts (and wearing his new Norfolk jacket 'perhaps a little more tightly belted than an Englishman would have worn it'), raises his gun but – and here I am reminded of my father – stops himself from firing just in time.

A smile seemed to be passed along the line in the wake of the animal. Tibor accordingly received it from Lionel Stephens and passed it on to Tommy Farmer, rather as if it were an item, a slipper perhaps, in one of those mysterious games which Cicely would insist on playing after dinner.

The roe deer is indulged, while the game birds are slaughtered in their hundreds.

But this book is much more than a description of the mores of wealthy Edwardians at play; the other side of the etiquette coin might be said to be duty. Sir Randolph is a landowner of the old school who feels fiercely responsible for his land, his tenants, his estate workers, his servants. He knows them all by name and is acquainted with their various circumstances; he knows when a roof needs mending and the man to do it, congratulating him on a job well done despite being aware that the man poaches regularly on his estate; when the gamekeeper's son Dan shows an interest in scientific study Sir Randolph offers to pay for his education. Hearing that a neighbouring landowner is thinking of letting out his estate, he fulminates:

'Of course he can't keep up with the costs, none of us can keep up with the costs. I'm mortgaged up to the hilt . . . Who's he found to let it to then? Some damned newspaper proprietor I suppose. Somebody who'll do nothing but entertain his friends from Town and not give a thought to his obligations. The countryside needs all the help it can get in times like this.'

Sir Randolph senses that he may be one of a dying breed but he worries for the future of the countryside, saying, 'If the landlord class goes, everything goes. It will be the ruin of rural England.' He does not (unlike Minnie, who is used to her luxuries) worry for himself, but he does grieve that the politicians are more concerned with urban issues than rural ones and he is well aware that the barbarians – in the shape of 'striking industrial workers, screaming suffragettes, Irish terrorists, scandals on the Stock Exchange, universal suffrage' – are at the gate.

Of course the reader knows that both the Edwardian code of etiquette and the paternalism of good landlords are about to be blown away in what Colegate bluntly calls 'a bigger shooting party . . . in Flanders'. We know too that houses with a full complement of servants are about to become a thing of the past. There is a wonderful scene in which Minnie confers with her head gardener while four men and a boy work in a nearby flowerbed; the thought of employing so many gardeners makes one's eyes water. When the guests stop for lunch on the third day of the shoot, their hosts contrive that they arrive at the boathouse; Minnie has had this converted to a 'rustic summerhouse' where the guests can sit down to lunch (beginning with lobster vol-au-vents and champagne) attended by the butler and two footmen, surrounded by comfortable furnishings, warmed by a log fire. And yet at this lunch Sir Randolph says to his neighbour, 'We are going to have a very different world, a world in which you and I . . . will each of us be dodos.'

There is much talk of change among the other characters, too; while there is affection for the old ways, the country rituals, there is also an undercurrent of questioning. Tom Harker, the poacher, talks of the 'stranglehold of the rich' and likes to quote Lloyd George. An anti-bloodsports campaigner appears on the scene and, although a confused and sometimes ludicrous character, does blurt out – at the most inopportune moment – 'If only I could make you see how utterly absurd you all are!' The beaters, the loaders, the men in the pub all talk about politics and, while most heartily distrust politicians, everyone seems to be engaged. No one actually knows war is coming but there is a definite sense that society is on the brink of change. In a brilliant use of dramatic irony, Colegate lets us overhear a heart-breaking conversation among some of the boys who are talking excitedly about their futures: one of them says, 'I may be going into the Army. It might be more fun.' And one of the more reflective guests compares the shoot to a military manoeuvre: 'We have bivouacked and are moving off now to the front line. War might be like this, casual, friendly and frightening.' It is this same guest who then privately wonders, 'Are we really all so beautiful and brave . . . or do we just think we are?'

Colegate introduces, and then confidently moves among, an array of fully drawn characters. We encounter the house-guests (an assortment of the socially confident and the insecure, the bright and the not-so-bright, the moral and the amoral), Sir Randolph's daughter-in-law and her four children, John the footman, Ellen the housemaid, Glass the gamekeeper, his son Dan, Harker the poacher and Cardew the campaigner. We are privy to fears, jealousies, ambitions and passions, all explored with careful understanding so that any judgements feel like the reader's own. The only character for whom the author shows scant sympathy is the one who commits that unforgivable breach of etiquette.

And then there is the duck. The duck, an important character in the sub-plot, appears early on in the drawing-room. A pet of Sir Randolph's grandson Osbert, it wanders in as the guests are having tea, suddenly becoming the centre of attention and providing an opportunity for some of the description at which Colegate excels:

> It opened its mouth in a sort of yawn – no sound emerged – it shut it again, shook its feathers slightly, then slowly extended one leg sideways as if in a dance movement. It then stretched one wing along the length of the leg, opening to view a patch of deep bright blue feathers barred with white which had been concealed beneath the speckled brown of its wing.

The fate of Osbert's duck is yet another source of the tension that builds during the course of this book, a page-turner describing characters you will care about, enacting a drama you will remember, in a glorious setting. It is a book built upon tensions (and not just because of all those loaded guns): not only the evident tensions between rich and poor, luxury and poverty, bloodlust and pacificism, but the tensions within each individual too and the private costs of heroism, altruism and virtue.

The Shooting Party is rich in meticulous description and a kaleidoscopic range of characters, but – poised at that moment of history as it is – it also asks big questions. Early on someone queries, 'Who says it's the height of heroism to kill? For every hero does there have to be a living sacrifice?' Gifted with hindsight, the reader can answer that. And, on the subject of society being forced to change, we witness Sir Randolph, many years later, sadly contemplating 'a sort of mass loss of memory, and the replacement of the common understandings of a civilized society by the destructive egotism of a barbaric one'.

Meanwhile, back in 1913 on the Nettleby estate, it is felt 'something must be going to happen'. Yes indeed.

POSY FALLOWFIELD's father was allowed to go out partridge-shooting with the neighbours (which was when he learnt it was only sporting to shoot a bird that was in flight); but those shoots were simple affairs, lunch being a hard-boiled egg out of his pocket.

Bedtime Stories

EWEN CAMPBELL

I can't remember if my parents read to me at bedtime. If they did, it left not a trace behind. They did, however, pack me off at the age of 13 to a traditional boarding-school where bedtime reading to the new boys' dormitory was an established ritual undertaken by the duty prefect. By the time I arrived this enlightened custom had degenerated from the originating housemaster's lofty ideals. Some of the prefects appeared, even to us, as barely literate. One would read two or three pages of whichever book came to hand. The following night his successor would repeat the process with a random extract from a different book. It was barely a system and did not lend itself to continuity. Some read fluently and with feeling. Some read to us in foreign languages, living and dead. It didn't matter. We adored it. It was a ritual and we were much aggrieved if it was denied. Perhaps that housemaster was wiser than I give him credit for. Perhaps even the prefects benefited.

Forty years ago I sat, for the first time, at the housemaster's desk in a traditional senior boarding-school myself. The wheel had come full circle. Loftily idealistic, I resolved to offer my fledglings a sophistication on my own experience, with the result that I was kept housebound every evening for the length of my tenure. (I imagine that, once this pattern was established, it was the cue for the rest of the house to decamp to their various hidey-holes and smoke themselves sick.)

Books that read well aloud benefit from a strong, page-turning plot and a handful of well-differentiated characters. My first choice was John le Carré's *A Murder of Quality* (1962) in which George

Smiley plays the detective following a murder at a posh traditional boarding-school called Carne. It is the only Smiley book which has nothing to do with espionage, but Smiley is as Smiley, methodically, does:

> It had been one of Smiley's cardinal principles in research, whether among the incunabula of an obscure poet or the laboriously gathered fragments of intelligence, not to proceed beyond the evidence . . . Accordingly he did not speculate with the remarkable discovery he had made but turned his mind to the most obscure problem of all: motive for murder.

My Smiley leaned heavily on the underplayed Alec Guinness version, while the catalogue of grotesques who make up the Senior Common Room of Carne offered ample scope for more extravagant characterization – the florid, hectoring Housemaster, for one, or the socially obsessed Shane Hecht for whom people exist 'to be found wanting in the minute tests of social behaviour, to be ridiculed, cut off, and destroyed', and who taunts Smiley, between the lines, over his wretched marriage. Add a hint of witchcraft in a vagrant madwoman who has witnessed the crime – 'Janey see'd him! Flying on the wind he was!' – then keep the clues coming and we all enjoyed a classic, pacy whodunnit, set close enough to home to have some listeners looking nervously over their shoulders.

Next came Geoffrey Household's *Watcher in the Shadows* (1960) which is darker in tone, begins with a convoluted mystery and accelerates to an enthralling midnight duel. Ten years after the war Charles Dennim, a retiring zoologist, suspects he is the intended victim when a letter-bomb kills the postman. His past in Intelligence, working undercover in the administration of a Nazi concentration camp, is revealed, but the identity of his assailant remains tantalizingly concealed. Cat-and-mouse manoeuvres, a blind game of chess, and a metaphorical goat tethered out in the open to lure the tiger take the plot deep into the English countryside as the hunter and the hunted are drawn psychologically and sympathetically towards each other. Near-misses and distant sightings engender a mutual respect which is finally and memorably resolved. Household deserves his reputation. *Watcher* is among his best.

The start of the second half of the Winter Term can be a low point. What more enjoyable palliative than Anthony Hope's *The Prisoner of Zenda* (1894), though I did wonder whether the Rudolph/Flavia love affair might lead to whispered accusations of 'soppiness'. How could I have doubted my audience? They homed in immediately on the conflicts of honour, duty and self-interest which – for all its derring-do, swordfights, midnight swims and narrow squeaks – provide the moral impetus that drives the plot. Invited by Hope to imagine ourselves transported to the throne of Ruritania, threatened with peril of discovery by a Black Michael hidebound by his own treachery, it is yet the spell of Flavia that pervades the book. Rudolph's final revelation and parting carry emotional heft:

> '*Rudolph – Flavia – always.*' That message, and the wearing of the rings, are all that now bind me to the Queen of Ruritania. For nobler as I hold her for the act, she has followed where her duty to her country and her house led her . . .

Reading aloud, I found Flavia a challenge, but Black Michael, Rupert, Fritz and Colonel Sapt come gift-wrapped. Each chapter takes thirteen minutes to read and ends with a cliff-hanger. Perfection. *King Solomon's Mines* (1885) is a quest story with tremendous scope, though somewhat dated for today's tastes. But Rider Haggard's narrator, the lantern-jawed ex-big game hunter Allan Quatermain is even-handed in his allowance of virtue as the only accolade:

> 'Am I a gentleman? . . . I've known natives who are, and so you will say, Harry my boy, before you've done with this tale, and I've known mean white men with lots of money and fresh out from home too, who are not.'

In an early exchange with Sir Henry Curtis, the organizer of the expedition to find his lost brother on which they embark, the native porter Umbopa philosophizes on the transience of life:

'It is the glow-worm that shines in the night-time and is black in the morning; it is the white breath of the oxen in winter; it is the little shadow that runs across the green and loses itself at sunset.'

'You are a strange man,' said Sir Henry when he had ceased.

Umbopa laughed. 'It seems to me we are much alike, Incubu. Perhaps I seek a brother over the mountains.'

And indeed he does. Once in Kukuana-land we are shown cruelty and self-sacrifice in full measure, interspersed with terrible dangers, unspeakable villainy, epic conflicts and a timely eclipse of the moon. It really is all here. And as the newly enriched adventurers, who have stumbled on the eponymous mines, return to 'civilization' they conveniently pick up Sir Henry's lost brother en route. *King Solomon's Mines* is the progenitor of the 'lost world' genre. Who wants realism?

A full-length Jeeves and Wooster lightens the mood and *Right Ho, Jeeves* (1934) provides the full range of Aunts, Drones, romantic misalliances and eccentrics. The cook, Anatole – 'God's gift to the gastric juices' – can 'take a few smooths with a rough' and so can Bertie, whose pitch-perfect narration here takes us through this alarming encounter with an owl on a signpost:

So agitated had my mind become at this time that I thought it was Aunt Agatha, and only when reason and reflection told me how alien to her habits it would be to climb signposts and sit on them, could I pull myself together and overcome the weakness.

My only problem was keeping a straight face.

The Summer Term, cricket matches, croquet, the onset of adolescence and (as little Leo wrote to his mother) 'grate heat' could lead only to L. P. Hartley's *The Go-Between* (1953) with its bitter-sweet cocktail of innocence, hopeless love, manipulation, betrayal, disappointment, deceit and catastrophe set against the backdrop of the social and emotional minefield of Brandham Hall. Don't go playing hopscotch there, Leo – you'll get hurt!

My reservation was to wonder whether we could carry off so rich and complex a work, but the younger Leo held their hands, and the older Leo mine, and on our various levels we got away with it.

Interspersed with many short stories these were the six novels that sustained us. They have stood the test of time, at least in my time, but times change and, as we are told, 'the past is a foreign country . . .'

EWEN CAMPBELL was a soldier, then a teacher, and is now a grower.

Bibliography

Coming attractions

GUSTAV TEMPLE is unnerved by Patricia Highsmith · DAISY
DUNN visits ancient Greece with Mary Renault · JUSTIN
MAROZZI takes a short walk in the Hindu Kush · ANNE
BOSTON falls for an Egyptian bestiary · ANTHONY WELLS
salutes Nadezhda Mandelstam · FRANCES DONNELLY meets
the real Lorin Jones · CHRIS SAUNDERS drops in on
Penelope Fitzgerald's bookshop